GOD

AND THE
BURDEN
OF PROOF

Frontiers of Philosophy
Peter H. Hare, Series Editor

Advisory Board

AND THE
BURDEN
OF PROOF

*PLANTINGA, SWINBURNE, AND
THE ANALYTIC DEFENSE OF THEISM*

KEITH M. PARSONS

PROMETHEUS BOOKS
Buffalo, New York

Published 1989 by Prometheus Books
700 East Amherst Street, Buffalo, New York 14215

Library of Congress Cataloging-in-Publication Data

Parsons, Keith M.
    God and the burden of proof / by Keith M. Parsons.
        p.   cm.
    Bibliography: p.
    Includes index.
    ISBN 0-87975-551-2
    1. God—Proof. 2. Theism. 3. Analysis (Philosophy) 4. Good and
evil. 5. Plantinga, Alvin—Contributions in doctrine of theism.
6. Swinburne, Richard—Contributions in doctrine of theism.
I. Title.
BT102.P312   1989
212′.1—dc 20   89-35013
                                                                    CIP

Printed on acid-free paper in the United States of America

To

Kay, Danny, and Erin,

whose love has meant more than they know

Foreword

The philosophy of religion in Anglo-American contexts has taken a curious turn in the past decade. During the turbulent sixties 'Death of God' theologies that pushed Paul Tillich farther than he would wish to be pushed became very fashionable indeed. We heard of 'Christian atheists' and 'Jewish atheists', though the atheism involved was arcane and elusive. In more sober analytical circles, philosophers such as Richard Braithwaite and R. M. Hare, both of whom claimed to be Christians, developed a philosophy of religion that in reality owed much to logical positivism. To believe in God was to be committed to a way of life (including a moral view of things) associated with certain stories that one might or might not believe. The distance of such views from the Judeo-Christian tradition is captured by Hare's remark that "the transcendent God is bound always to be an idle element in our religious life." (This, remember, is a Christian speaking, not a secular humanist.) Religion thus became, for people like Braithwaite and Hare, morality touched by emotion. In substance, though certainly not in idiom, very similar things came from those analytic philosophers, deeply influenced by Wittgenstein, whom I have called Wittgensteinian Fideists. From them we heard a lot about religious language and about the unique, *sui generis* language game or cluster of language games that is religion. The thing to do, they gave us to understand, is to come to understand these language games from the inside. When this is achieved, the claim went, we will see that they are in order just as they are. Arguments concerning God's existence or the problem of evil will then be seen to be pointless. If one has the appropriate needs and one comes to understand these language games in their actual settings in a way that a participant does, then one will also understand that there can be no intellectual problem about the viability of religious belief. One will also understand that there is no room for arguments between belief and unbelief. Here Kierkegaard and Wittgenstein work in harness. Finally there were analytic theologians, such as John Hick and Basil Mitchell, who accepted what they took to be the basic methods of analytic philosophy and the underlying tenets of empiricism but thought religion, including belief in God in a rather more robust sense than Braithwaite or Hare would allow, could be defended within a fundamentally empiricist framework.

All of these movements have fallen out of favor. They were, of course, vigorously criticized both by secularist philosophers and by traditional Christian philosophers and theologians. But whatever the cause of their demise, they are no longer at the forefront of the debate in the philosophy of religion. What has come to the forefront— and this is where Keith Parsons's tale begins—is a group of Christian philosophers of a philosophically analytical persuasion, but hostile to even the residues of logical empiricism or Wittgensteinianism, who return to the old topics and the old theses of traditional Christian philosophy and natural theology. This seems to me a boring and unfortunate turning back of the clock, as if Hume, Kant, and Kierkegaard had never written and the intellectual history of the last two hundred years had been forgotten. These Christian philosophers would no doubt see their return to tradition, while remaining loyal to the ideals of analytic philosophy, as just an escape from the dogmas of empiricism and pragmatism. On the contrary, I think it shows a failure to take to heart, for all their errors, what these forms of empiricism and naturalism have achieved. Be that as it may, these philosophers have become a force in 'philosophy of religion circles', and the most important of their members are Alvin Plantinga and Richard Swinburne. This movement and these philosophers in particular need to be assessed from a secular humanist perspective. This Keith Parsons has done with dedication, integrity, and intelligence. After setting the stage for such a discussion, he then patiently and accurately elucidates and critiques Plantinga; then he turns with a similar patience and perceptiveness to an elucidation and critique of Swinburne who, far more than Plantinga, chances his arm. The result is a renewed argument—dialogue, if you will—between belief and unbelief, which, while written in a straightforward and nontechnical style, takes us into the heartland of arguments that are now, for good or for ill, in the forefront of the philosophy of religion. (I said 'forefront' not 'cutting edge'. Philosophy of religion may have no cutting edge.)

Kai Nielsen
The University of Calgary

Preface

Late in the nineteenth century, a dense metaphysical fog settled on British universities. Under the influence of Immanuel Kant and G. W. H. Hegel, leading British philosophers such as F. H. Bradley and J. M. E. McTaggart began to say things that would have sounded very strange to Thomas Hobbes, John Locke, David Hume, or John Stuart Mill. They said that reality was a single, undivided whole and that all appearance of plurality was an illusion. They said that nothing is absolutely true or false, but only more or less so or not so. They denied the reality of time and matter. The universe, they claimed, only exists because we are here to perceive it.

Two young Cambridge philosophers, G. E. Moore and Bertrand Russell, led a rebellion against such metaphysics. Russell describes this rebellion and the sense of liberation it produced:

> During 1898, various things caused me to abandon both Kant and Hegel. . . . But these motives would have operated more slowly than they did, but for the influence of G. E. Moore. He also had had a Hegelian period, but it was briefer than mine. He took the lead in rebellion, and I followed, with a sense of emancipation. Bradley argued that everything common sense believes is mere appearance; we reverted to the opposite extreme, and thought *everything* is real that common sense, uninfluenced by philosophy or theology, supposes real. With a sense of escaping from prison, we allowed ourselves to think that

11

grass is green, that the sun and stars would exist if no one was aware of them. . . . The world, which had been thin and logical, suddenly became rich and varied and solid. Mathematics could be *quite* true, and not merely a stage in dialectic.[1]

Thus the analytic tradition in philosophy began—with a sense of liberation from dogma, mysticism, subjectivism, and muddle-headedness. With Russell and Moore, clarity and precision became the norms of good thinking, rather than weighty jargon and ponderous obscurity. Philosophers could enjoy a robust sense of reality; they could trust their senses and natural science to inform them about an external, objectively existing world.

The analytic tradition founded by Moore and Russell has had a worldwide influence.[2] In the English-speaking world it became the dominant mode of philosophizing, and remains so despite the fact that its hegemony has weakened in the last decade or so.

Of course, analytic philosophy has undergone many changes since its beginning. Many of today's analytic philosophers would demur at Russell and Moore's ringing affirmations of commonsense realism and the objectivity of knowledge. However, in many ways analytic philosophy has remained true to its roots. Vagueness, imprecision, and obscurity masquerading as profundity are not tolerated.

The demand for exactness and clarity has led to the extensive employment of the powerful tools of symbolic logic within analytic philosophy. Symbolic logic—the mathematical science that grew out of the traditional and less formal logic that preceded it—has grown to maturity in this century. Analytic philosophers such as Russell, C. I. Lewis, W. V. O. Quine, and Saul Kripke have been seminal figures in the development of the field. The various branches of symbolic logic are now employed by analytic philosophy to elucidate many traditional areas of philosophical interest.

Another typical characteristic of analytic philosophy is its emphasis upon the analysis of language. Its philosophical adherents realized early on that only by strictly minding our language can we hope to avoid confusion and ambiguity. They realized that our intellects are often bewitched by the misuse of language and that such bewitchment makes effective, logical thinking impossible.[3] Hence, they concluded that one of the major tasks of philosophy is to make clear the structure, nature, and functions of language.

Because they prize clear and precise language so highly, analytic philosophers are sharply critical of language that they consider vague, mysterious, or incoherent. For instance, some have charged that core religious utterances, such as those found in the traditional creeds, are meaningless, incoherent, or devoid of cognitive significance. Kai Nielsen is perhaps the best known proponent of the view that central bits of God-talk fail to meet minimal standards of coherence.[4] Since the coherence of religious language has been thoroughly discussed by Nielsen and others, it will not be treated here.[5]

Analytic philosophers also challenge traditional theism by placing a much greater burden of logical rigor on the defender of theistic truth-claims. The standard theistic "proofs" have been subjected to searching and incisive criticisms by such analytic philosophers as J. L. Mackie and Antony Flew.[6] Further, such philosophers have produced sophisticated formulations of traditional difficulties plaguing theism, e.g., the problem of evil. To meet such criticisms—if they can be met—will require logical acumen and technical expertise of a very high order.

Recently, a number of analytic philosophers possessing the requisite skills have come forward to defend traditional theism. The purpose of this book is to provide an introductory examination of recent attempts to defend traditional theism within the context of analytic philosophy. Some such attempts, most notably those of Alvin Plantinga and Richard Swinburne, are the focus of much current debate in the philosophy of religion. Unfortunately, these debates are frequently couched in a highly technical idiom that makes them inaccessible to many students and interested laypersons. For instance, Plantinga makes use of the formidable technical machinery of possible-worlds semantics and Swinburne bases his arguments on Bayesian confirmation theory. Hence, there is a need for a work that presents these issues to nonspecialists in as perspicuous and nontechnical a manner as possible. This work aims to meet that need. Further, I intend to make a critical evaluation, from a secular humanist perspective, of some of the most important arguments of the theistic analytic philosophers.

This book will take the two philosophers mentioned above—Plantinga and Swinburne—as representative defenders of traditional theism. Since these two philosophers have published voluminously on a large number of topics, just a very few of their major arguments will be examined. The reason for placing such severe restrictions on the scope of the topics examined is that this book is intended to be brief, as indicated above, and is directed to an uninitiated audience. It is my firm conviction that a great deal more is learned when a few issues are explored in depth than when a large number of topics is examined superficially.

There are two reasons for selecting Plantinga and Swinburne as representative defenders of theism: First, the sheer volume of response and comment by other philosophers indicates that they are influential and highly regarded theistic philosophers. Second, though they are both defenders of traditional theism, Plantinga and Swinburne develop their defenses in widely divergent ways. Indeed, they are very different both in their general philosophical orientations and in their positions on specific issues. Hence, by studying them together it is possible to compare, contrast, and evaluate two very different modes of the philosophical defense of theism.

Philosophy of religion is seldom the first course students take in the field of philosophy. It is usually offered at the junior or senior level: one can assume, therefore, that a few prior courses in philosophy have been taken. Hence, I have not stopped to explain the most basic terms. I assume that readers are familiar with such terms as "inductive," "deductive," "epistemology," "a priori," and "a posteriori." However, I have endeavored not to presuppose any knowledge beyond what a student could be expected to have learned in an introductory logic course and a course in introductory philosophy.

Like all branches of analytic philosophy, the analytic philosophy of religion is a highly technical field. However, as books such as Heinz Pagels's *The Cosmic Code* have shown, even so arcane a subject as quantum physics can be made comprehensible if explained skillfully. While I have endeavored to present this material as lucidly as possible, I have also been careful not to oversimplify. This would be a disservice to the reader and a discourtesy to those whose positions I discuss.

I have organized the issues discussed in this book around a fairly well-known theme: Which side must bear the burden of proof in debates between theists and atheists? In the first chapter I examine Plantinga's claim that there is no special burden of proof that must be borne by theists. He argues that theistic belief is perfectly rational even if theists can offer no arguments, reasons, or evidence for their belief. Swinburne, on the other hand, is perfectly willing to concede that theists must shoulder the burden of proof. Further, he offers arguments that attempt to meet that burden. The second chapter will examine and evaluate one of Swinburne's main arguments. In the third chapter the tables are turned to ascertain whether atheists can bear the burden of proof in arguing against theism. I shall ask whether the existence of evil provides any grounds for disbelief in the existence of God.

Now for some definitions: The terms "theist," "atheist," and "agnostic" have traditionally been construed to apply to those who respectively affirm, deny, and suspend judgment concerning the existence of God. Such usage is still presupposed by a number of writers, including Norwood Russell Hanson, whose views are examined early in chapter 1. I prefer the usage, advocated by Antony Flew, in which "theist" means "one who believes in God" and "atheist" means simply "one who lacks belief in God." One can lack belief in God without being in a position to *deny* God's existence. Hence, except where otherwise noted, "atheist" will simply mean "nontheist" and not "one who denies the existence of God."

I would like to take this opportunity to thank those whose assistance on this project has been greatly appreciated. First, I would like to thank my editor, Steven L. Mitchell of Prometheus Books, for his patience in awaiting my manuscript while I battled a crushing teaching load and a 140-mile commute. I would also like to thank the members of a philosophy of religion study group consisting of Robert Arrington, Associate Dean of Arts and Sciences, Georgia State University, and my colleagues in the GSU Department of Philosophy: David Blumenfeld, Jim Humber, Mark Wallace, and Tim Renick. I learned much from the lively discussions and debates we enjoyed. Without the aid of the members of this group my understanding of the issues discussed in this book would have been significantly diminished.

I would also like to thank Robert Almeder and Mark Wallace for their reading of portions of the manuscript and their perspicacious comments and criticisms. Thanks are also due to my doctoral dissertation supervisor, Dr. Carlos Prado of Queen's University, Ontario, Canada. Since much of this book has evolved from ideas first presented in my dissertation, Dr. Prado's supervision of that work also guided the development of the present book.

Thanks are especially due to Professor Kai Nielsen of the University of Calgary, Alberta, Canada, for his invaluable aid in bringing this project to the attention of Prometheus Books and for his kind offer to write a Foreword. I was a great admirer of Dr. Nielsen's work long before I began my doctoral studies. To have the aid and encouragement of a philosopher of his stature has been an enormous inspiration.

Finally, I would like to thank my father, Arthur W. Parsons, and my sister, Kay P. Beavers, for giving in to my importunate requests to read or listen to long sections of this manuscript. Their perceptive comments and questions have assured me that intelligent nonphilosophers can find the analytic philosophy of religion to be comprehensible and, indeed, fascinating.

One final note: I have made no special effort to meet the stylistic dictates of currently fashionable "inclusive" or "nonsexist" usage. I find such constructions as "he or she" and "he/she" and "(s)he" barbarous. Further, I find it distracting and irritating when a writer mechanically switches back and forth between masculine and feminine pronouns. Hence, I frequently retain the traditional use of the masculine pronoun when my intention is to refer to persons in general regardless of gender. I sincerely hope that when I do so I will not be construed as referring exclusively to males.

NOTES

1. Bertrand Russell, "My Mental Development," in *The Philosophy of Bertrand Russell,* ed. Paul Arthur Schilpp (New York: Harper and Row, 1963), pp. 11–12.

2. For a history of the rise and development of analytic philosophy see John Passmore's two books, *A Hundred Years of Philosophy* (New York: Basic Books, 1966), and *Recent Philosophers* (LaSalle, Ill.: Open Court, 1985).

3. This was the theme of much of Ludwig Wittgenstein's later philosophy. See his *Philosophical Investigations* (New York: Macmillan, 1968).

4. See Kai Nielsen, *Contemporary Critiques of Religion* (New York: Macmillan, 1971); *Skepticism* (New York: Macmillan, 1973); and *Philosophy and Atheism* (Buffalo, N.Y.: Prometheus Books, 1985).

5. See also Richard Swinbure, *The Coherence of Theism* (Oxford, England: Oxford University Press, 1977).

6. See J. L. Mackie, *The Miracle of Theism* (Oxford, England: Clarendon Press, 1982), and Antony Flew, *God and Philosophy* (London: Hutchinson, 1966).

Contents

1

Plantinga and the Rationality of Theism

A well-known anecdote about Bertrand Russell tells of the time he was asked what he, the notorious agnostic, would say if after death he were ushered into the presence of God and commanded to account for his unbelief. Russell, with characteristic aplomb, replied. "I'd say 'Not enough evidence, God! Not enough evidence!' "[1]

The Apostle Paul, who would doubtless be horrified at Russell's flippancy in the presence of the Almighty, would be unwilling to accept the excuse of insufficient evidence. Saint Paul held that the ungodly cannot excuse their wickedness with a plea of ignorance of God's existence:

> For all that may be known of God by men lies plain before their eyes; indeed God himself has disclosed it to them. His invisible attributes, that is to say his everlasting power and deity, have been visible, ever since the world began, to the eye of reason, in the things he has made. There is therefore no possible defense of their [ungodly persons'] conduct; knowing God, they have refused to honor him as God, or to render him thanks. (Rom. 1:19-21, *The New English Bible*)

In other words, since God's existence and attributes, made manifest in his works, are plainly visible to the eye of reason, no rational person can fail to acknowledge the reality of God.

How is it then that so many apparently rational people, like

Russell, have claimed to be unbelievers? The answer that Saint Paul appears to endorse is that such persons have allowed sin to eclipse their rational faculties to such an extent that they deny the obvious truth of God's existence.

But *is* God's existence so plainly visible to the "eye of reason"? Is it, as Saint Paul appears to indicate, a simple and obvious step to infer God's existence from consideration of the universe ("the things he has made")? Were Confucius, the Buddha, Aristotle, Spinoza, and Einstein so mired in sin that they refused to make that simple and obvious inference? It would have been helpful if Saint Paul had given an argument in support of his claim.

However, the claim that something is obvious seems to be a hard one to argue for. How is one to reply to someone who says "Well, it isn't obvious to *me*"? There seems to be no way to argue that someone does find something obvious so long as he consistently speaks and acts as though he does not. Further, how could Saint Paul respond to the counterclaim that it is just obvious that the existence of God is *not* obvious for everyone?

Most theistic philosophers have, at least in practice, disagreed with Saint Paul and have regarded God's existence as less than patently obvious to everyone. To deal with skeptics such as Russell, and to provide support for their own faith, such philosophers developed the field of natural theology.

Natural theology stands in contrast to revealed theology. The latter presupposes the existence of a definitive revelation (e.g., the Torah, the Gospels, or the Qur'ran) and attempts to interpret or understand the implications of that purported revelation. Natural theology, on the other hand, aims to employ only the "natural light" of human reason (i.e., reason unaided by revelation or divine inspiration) to establish God's existence and possession of certain attributes. Natural theology typically draws upon premises taken as self-evident (such as that nothing exists unless there is a sufficient reason for its existence), or those of a very general and widely accepted sort (such as that the universe exists). Such premises are taken as proving, or at least strongly supporting, theistic claims.

The traditional ontological, cosmological, and teleological arguments for God's existence are the classical products of natural theology. Unfortunately for natural theologians, these arguments—or at least the traditional versions of them—have received rough treatment at the hands of skeptical philosophers. As a result of the failure (or perceived failure) of these arguments, theologians have increasingly turned away from natural theology.

Some atheists have seen the movement away from natural theology as a capitulation on the part of theists. That is, they see the abandonment of natural theology as tantamount to the admission that no case can be made for theistic belief. Such atheists therefore challenge theists to "put up or shut up." They challenge theists either to provide cogent arguments for God's existence or to surrender any claim to the truth or superior rationality of theism. This challenge, known as the "evidentialist challenge," is a mainstay of much recent atheist argument.[2] Indeed, it forms such an integral part of the atheist critique of theism that theistic philosophy of religion can hardly progress unless that challenge is met or obviated. Hence, we turn now to an examination of the evidentialist challenge.

Perhaps the most forceful presentation of this challenge to theism—certainly the one carried off with the most style and panache—is found in Norwood Russell Hanson's essay "What I Don't Believe."[3] Early on Hanson tells us that the existence of God is certainly something that *could* be established beyond all reasonable doubt. Indeed, he finds it easy to imagine a circumstance that would convince him:

> Suppose . . . that on next Tuesday morning, just after our breakfast, all of us in this one world are knocked to our knees by a percussive and ear-shattering thunderclap. Snow swirls; leaves drop from trees; the earth heaves and buckles; buildings topple and towers tumble; the sky is ablaze with an eerie, silvery light. Just then, as all the people of this world look up, the heavens open—the clouds pull apart—revealing an unbelievably immense and radiant Zeus-like figure, towering up above us like a hundred Everests. He frowns darkly as lightning plays across the features of his Michaelangeloid face. He then points down—at me!—and exclaims, for every man, woman, and child to hear: "I have had quite enough of your too-clever logic-chopping and word-watching in matters of theology. Be assured, N. R. Hanson, that I do most certainly exist."[4]

Needless to say, such a Spielbergian display would fill the churches to overflowing with former atheists; Hanson himself would undoubtedly be in the front pew. However, says Hanson, no such remarkable revelatory event has ever befallen him. Moreover, he sees no reason to think that any such event has ever occurred.

What reason, then, can there be for believing in God? The various traditional "proofs" of God's existence are notorious failures, Hanson claims. Further, God's existence is not supported by scientific evidence of the sort that leads physicists to infer the existence of force fields or subatomic particles. Theism does not appear to yield any empirically testable predictions that would allow for its experimental confirmation.

According to Hanson, therefore, belief in God is not grounded in any clear and authoritative revelation; neither is it supported by cogent argument or compelling evidence. Hanson concludes that there is no good reason for belief in the existence of God.[5]

Hanson notes that whenever he has had occasion to voice the above conclusion—at cocktail parties, say—it has almost always provoked the same, usually angry, retort: "Well, can *you* prove that God does *not* exist?" Hanson tells us how the conversation typically proceeds from that point:

> And when, as experience and puzzlement have taught me always to do, I decline even to gesture at such a proof such an enthusiast smiles triumphantly 'round at the relieved believers there in attendance, as if he were Saint George and the dragon of disbelief were now dead from his dialectical dart.[6]

However, says Hanson, the retort of the "cocktail party St. George" misses the point:

> There is no proof (in George's sense) that green goblins do not exist on the far side of the moon. There is no proof that a blue Brontosaurus does not exist in Brazil. There is no proof that the Loch Ness monster does not exist. But the nonexistence of such proofs does not give us the slightest reason for supposing that goblins, Brontosaura, or monsters *do* exist! In this sense of "proof" (St. George's), there can never be a proof that Shangri-La does not exist. Or that the Abominable Snowman does not exist! Or that Flying Saucers do not exist! Nonetheless, anyone who inferred from the absence of *this* kind of proof that there *was* good reason therefore to suppose that Shangri-La, the Abominable Snowman and Flying Saucers *do* exist, such a one would have badly confused two radically different senses of the expression "Proved the existence of X."[7]

What "St. George" is demanding is that Hanson provide a formal, deductive disproof of God's existence—a disproof of the sort mathematicians use to disprove the existence of a greatest prime number or to show that there cannot exist a fraction equivalent to pi. Such disproofs show that something *cannot* exist. Indeed, to disprove the existence of X in this way is to show that we cannot even *conceive* that X exists without generating contradictions or logical paradoxes.

Hanson, on the other hand, claims that our concept of God is a concept of a being of the sort that philosophers call "contingent." Contingent beings are those that can be conceived either to exist or not to exist without generating any contradictions or logical paradoxes. If a contingent being exists, it always makes sense to suppose that it might not have existed. Likewise, if a contingent being does not exist, it always makes sense to suppose that it might have existed. Clearly, contingent beings cannot be proven not to exist in the same way that the greatest prime number can be proven not to exist. Therefore, it is inappropriate for "St. George" to demand such a disproof of God's existence. To disprove the existence of a contingent being requires a different type of argument.

Detailed examples are needed to make clearer the two types of disproof mentioned above. Mathematical proofs, such as Euclid's marvelous proof of the nonexistence of a greatest prime number, are a little hard for the nonmathematically inclined to follow. Therefore, as an instance of such formal, deductive disproof, let us consider Bertrand Russell's disproof of the existence of a certain type of barber. Suppose that in a certain village there is a barber who is himself a resident of that village, who shaves *all* and *only* those villagers who do not shave themselves. Now ask the following question: "Does the barber shave himself?" It is impossible to answer either yes or no. If we say yes, then the barber does shave himself. But we said above that the barber shaves *only* those who do *not* shave themselves. Hence, if we say that the barber does shave himself, we are forced in the next breath to say that he does not! Suppose, then, we say that the barber does *not* shave himself. But then it follows that the barber *does* shave himself since we said above that he shaves *all* those villagers who do not shave themselves. Hence, if the barber does shave himself, he doesn't and if he doesn't, he does! Since the supposition that there could be such a barber thus generates unresolvable paradoxes, we must reject that supposition and conclude that no such barber can exist.

What Hanson's "St. George" is demanding is a similar disproof of God's existence. Such a disproof would show that the supposition of God's existence generates logical paradoxes or self-contradictions of the sort generated by supposing that Russell's barber exists. In other words, such a disproof would show that God's existence is impossible.

Now some atheists have attempted to provide just such disproofs of God's existence.[8] Hanson does not think it possible to give such a disproof. That is, he does not think that the supposition of God's existence generates logical paradoxes in the way that supposing the existence of Russell's barber does.

Hanson's "disproof" of the existence of God is an entirely different kind of argument. Instead of being like the argument against the existence of Russell's barber, it is more like the kind of argument we might make to show that no barbers exist who still charge only twenty-five cents for a shave. The barber who still charges twenty-five cents for a shave can be supposed to exist without generating any logical paradoxes. Unlike Russell's barber, it is perfectly possible that a barber could exist who only charges twenty-five cents for a shave. In fact, such barbers *did* exist just a few decades ago. How, then, do we establish that, as a matter of fact, there are no more barbers who charge twenty-five cents for a shave?

By looking and seeing, says Hanson.[9] Suppose we make a thorough survey of all the barber shops in our town and find that they all charge more than twenty-five cents for a shave. We would then have very solid grounds for claiming that in our town no barbers exist who charge twenty-five cents for a shave.

The same sort of look-and-see approach would apply to the assessment of more extraordinary claims, such as the claims made by those who say that flying saucers, the Loch Ness monster, or the Abominable Snowman exist. Surely, such things can be supposed to exist without generating any logical paradoxes or self-contradictions; that is, such things *could* conceivably exist. We evaluate claims that they *do* in fact exist by examining the evidence. If no evidence is found in support of such claims, rational persons will reject those claims. Indeed, rational persons will *deny* the existence of flying saucers, monsters, ghosts, etc., if there is no evidence whatsoever *for* such supposed entities. If, for instance, careful and thorough sonar searches fail to detect Nessie, the only reasonable conclusion is that Nessie doesn't exist.

Indeed, says Hanson, there are only two ways to show the non-existence of something. One way is to prove that it cannot exist, i.e., that the supposition that it does exist leads to logical paradoxes or inconsistencies. This is the way to prove the nonexistence of Russell's barber, the greatest prime number, round squares, married bachelors, and all other such things that cannot exist. However, for things that could exist but, as a matter of fact, do not, there can only be one way to show their nonexistence—by carefully looking and seeing.

Having gotten clear on the two different senses of "proving the nonexistence of something," Hanson is finally ready to respond to "St. George's" demand for a disproof of God's existence.

> The lack of any conclusive, formal (deductive) proof that God does not exist provides no reason whatever for supposing that God *does* exist. On the contrary, a "proof" that God does *not* exist might very well be felt to be the name of that enterprise which consists in reviewing all the proferred [sic] reasons which purport to show that God does exist, and then demonstrating that none of those reasons are *good* reasons. Thus, just as we prove that a bike has not been stolen by revealing that there is no good reason for supposing that it *has been* (e.g., by opening the garage door and disclosing the bike itself), so also it could be argued that a proof that God does *not* exist turns on no more than the demonstration that there is no good reason whatever for supposing that he *does* exist.[10]

In other words, for Hanson the claim that God does not exist is much like the claim that Hobbits, witches, Santa Claus, the Bermuda Triangle, and honest politicians do not exist. All these latter entities certainly could conceivably exist. However, the utter lack of evidence or any other good reason for holding that such things *do* exist gives us excellent grounds for *denying* their existence. According to Hanson, the same holds for the claim that God exists. To show that no compelling evidence or cogent argument can be offered in support of God's existence is tantamount to showing that God does *not* exist.

Hanson anticipates an objection to his position.[11] He expects that some persons will maintain that lack of evidence for something only justifies the suspension of belief with respect to claims that such a thing exists. According to such persons, usually termed "agnostics," lack of evidence for something does not justify the outright denial of the existence of that thing. Hence, so the agnostic's objection goes, Hanson is unjustified in saying that the lack of argument or evidence in favor of God's existence provides grounds for denying that God exists. According to the agnostic, Hanson should suspend judgment with respect to the question of God's existence, i.e., he should neither believe nor disbelieve but should refrain from committing himself to either position.

However, says Hanson, the agnostic can only maintain his pose of being perfectly suspended between belief and disbelief by illicitly shifting his logical ground. The agnostic starts by agreeing with Hanson that God's existence, like the existence of UFOs, the Lost Continent of Atlantis, etc., is something that needs to be established with evidence. He further agrees with Hanson that such evidence is lacking and thus that we should not believe that God exists. However, says Hanson, the agnostic then shifts his ground by siding with "St. George" in demanding a formal, deductive disproof of God's existence before committing himself to a denial.

But the agnostic cannot have it both ways, Hanson continues. Either God is the sort of being whose existence *could* be established by the appropriate evidence or he is not. If God is the former sort of being, as the agnostic maintains, then his *nonexistence* would be established in the same way, i.e., by examining the evidence. The lack of a formal, deductive disproof of the existence of such a being would be totally irrelevant to the question of whether or not it exists.

What is relevant to establishing the nonexistence of such a being is the total lack of any good reason for thinking that there is such a being. Indeed,

> . . . if looking and not finding does not constitute grounds for denying the existence of God, then looking and not finding does not constitute grounds for denying the existence of goblins, witches, devils, five-headed Welshmen, Unicorns, mermaids, Loch Ness monsters, flying saucers, Hobbits, Santa Claus . . . etc. *But there are excellent grounds for denying the existence of such entities.* They consist not simply in the failure to find and identify such remarkable creatures. Rather, these grounds consist largely in the fact that there is no good reason whatsoever for supposing that such creatures *do* exist.[12]

It therefore seems that the agnostic, unless he is willing to suspend judgment rather than deny the existence of the Great Pumpkin, the Easter Bunny, the Tooth Fairy, etc., should also be willing to deny the existence of God.

In summary, the evidentialist challenge, as presented by Hanson, runs as follows: Theists make an extraordinary claim when they say that God exists. It is a claim very much like those made by persons who assert the existence of Bigfoot, the Bermuda Triangle, poltergeists, the Loch Ness monster, and all other such alleged paranormal entities. Such things surely *could* exist; their existence cannot be disproved in the way that Euclid disproved the existence of a greatest prime number. How, then, do we determine whether such things do in fact exist?

A patient, fair, and open-minded examination of the purported evidence for such entities seems to be the only way to confirm or disconfirm their existence. If we find solid evidence for the existence of, say, Bigfoot—perhaps a scientific expedition providing clear, un-retouched photos of a colony of Bigfoots (Bigfeet?) happily foraging—then skeptics should humbly admit that they were wrong. If, on the other hand, the years pass by and expeditions fail to capture a Bigfoot, trappers fail to trap one, hunters fail to bag one, shutterbugs fail to produce not-obviously-faked photographs of one, what are we to conclude? Is it reasonable to suspend judgment indefinitely? No, Hanson would say, a rational person will eventually reach the point where the repeated failure of efforts to come up with acceptable evidence for Bigfoot will finally lead him to conclude that there is no such thing.

According to Hanson, the evidential situation with respect to God is much like that with respect to Bigfoot. Centuries, indeed millennia, of effort on the part of apologists, theologians, and theistic philosophers have failed to turn up any acceptable argument or evidence for the existence of God. Further, God is not presupposed by any of the sciences; they continue to flourish on the basis of purely naturalistic assumptions. Indeed, nothing in our lives seems more explicable or more comprehensible on the assumption that God exists. Finally, no thundering, Spielbergian, Zeus-like figures appear in the heavens; no "raptures" or Second Comings have been observed; and the stars do not rearrange themselves to spell out "PREPARE TO MEET THY GOD!" Since, therefore, as with Bigfoot, repeated efforts have failed to provide any objective, unambiguous, publicly available evidence for the existence of God, Hanson concludes that God does not exist.

As indicated earlier, other philosophers have developed their own versions of the evidentialist challenge. Michael Scriven's version is very much like Hanson's but is even harsher in its judgment of theism's position vis-à-vis the evidence. As Scriven notes, at least Bigfoot and the Loch Ness monster are not alleged to possess any powers or attributes of an utterly unprecedented sort.[13] Presumably, they are flesh-and-blood creatures with anatomies, physiologies, and habits that don't differ too much from those of creatures already known. Therefore, says Scriven, it is not altogether improbable that there could be such creatures.

However, Scriven notes that the situation is different when it is being claimed that something exists with powers and attributes of a sort very different from the ones we have previously encountered. When a claim asserts the existence of something that is greatly at odds with our previous experience, we rightly regard the claim as very probably false until we are given truly strong evidence in its favor. Thus, we are not too skeptical when, in reading the newspaper, we find that the world high-jump record has been exceeded by a centimeter or two. However, we would indeed be very skeptical, and rightly so, if we read (anywhere but in the comic pages) that someone had leapt a tall building at a single bound. The same would hold for claims that human beings exist who can foretell the future, move large objects telekinetically, perform miraculous cures, or fly simply by flapping their arms. All of our knowledge about human capacities and abilities counts against such claims.

The relevance of these considerations to theistic claims is obvious. All of God's alleged powers and attributes are of a very extraordinary sort. As defined by orthodox theists, God is not constituted of energy or matter, he does not exist in space and time (though he can act in space and time), and he created the universe though he himself is uncreated. Further, God is said to be all-powerful, all-knowing, and perfectly good. Clearly, as theists themselves insist, God is entirely different from the finite, limited, imperfect, material sorts of beings that we encounter in the natural world. Therefore, if we are to judge how likely something is to exist on the basis of what we have previously known to be the case, we must rate the likelihood of God's existence very low indeed. Further, since extraordinary claims must be supported with extraordinary evidence, we must insist on very solid evidence indeed before we affirm the existence of God.

Scriven concludes that atheism is obligatory if there is no adequate evidence for the existence of God.[14] He then examines the various arguments for God's existence and claims that neither singly nor in conjunction do they give good reason to believe in God.

Antony Flew's version of the evidentialist objection is somewhat different. Flew begins by proposing that we redefine the word 'atheist'.[15] Instead of meaning 'one who denies the existence of God', Flew proposes that it mean 'one who is not a theist'. In other words, for Flew an atheist is simply a nontheist—one who does not possess a belief in God's existence. It is possible to be an atheist in Flew's sense without denying the existence of God. The agnostic who suspends belief with respect to the question of God's existence, the Papuan tribesman who has never heard of God, and the newborn infant who cannot yet understand talk about God are all atheists on Flew's definition. Clearly, such persons are not in a position to deny God's existence. They are atheists on Flew's definition because they lack belief in God and therefore are not theists.

With atheism thus 'negatively' defined, Flew now asks how debate should proceed between theists and atheists. In any debate it is important to ascertain on whom the burden of proof must fall. That is, when two parties disagree over the truth of a proposition, it must be determined whether the side that supports that proposition has the responsibility of proving it true or whether the side that opposes it must prove it false. Usually, that responsibility is evenly divided between the two parties of a dispute. Suppose, for instance, that the issue being debated is whether Congress should act to ban all handguns. In such a debate it would appear that one side has the responsibility of showing that Congress should so act, and the other side has the burden of showing that Congress should not enact such legislation.

Sometimes, however, the burden of proof falls more heavily on one side of a debate than the other. Indeed, there are times when one side has to bear the whole burden of proof. In such a case, one side has the responsibility of proving its claim but the other side does not have the same responsibility of proving the opposing claim. The side that does not bear the burden of proof only has the responsibility of refuting the arguments offered by the side that does. For instance, in a court of law the defendant is presumed innocent until proven guilty. This means that the burden of proof falls on the prosecution rather than on the defense. That is, the defendant does not have the responsibility of proving his innocence (after all, hs is *presumed* innocent); all he has to do is refute the prosecution's claim to have proven him guilty "beyond a reasonable doubt."

Flew contends that this same sort of situation ought to hold in debates between theists and atheists. He argues that a presumption of atheism should govern the debate between theists and atheists just as the presumption of innocence rules over the debate between defense and prosecution. That is, Flew holds that theists must bear the burden of proof in their debates with atheists. This means that unless theists support with cogent arguments their claim that God exists, atheism will be presumed to have carried the day. Atheists, according to Flew, do not have the responsibility of proving God's nonexistence; all they have to do is refute the arguments proffered by theists.

Why should theists be willing to accept such a burden of proof? Why should they agree to a rule that ostensibly puts them at an initial disadvantage in the debate? Flew justifies his presumption of atheism by reminding us of the difference between knowledge and true belief:

> Knowledge involves true belief; not all true belief constitutes knowledge. To have a true belief is simply and solely to believe that something is so, and to be in fact right. But someone may believe that this or that is so, and his belief may in fact be true, without its thereby and necessarily constituting knowledge. If a true belief is to achieve this more elevated status, then the believer has to be properly warranted so to believe. He must, that is, be in a position to know.[16]

In other words, any claim to possess knowledge must be grounded. It must be backed up with reasons, arguments, or evidence that warrant the belief that what is claimed is in fact so. Flew continues:

> It is by reference to this inescapable demand for grounds that the presumption of atheism is justified. If it is to be established that there is a God, then we have to have good grounds for believing that this is indeed so. Until and unless some such grounds are produced we have literally no reason at all for believing.[17]

It therefore seems that, insofar as theists claim to know that God exists, they must be willing to back that claim with grounds adequate to justify that belief. A curious observer might wonder why atheists are not required to shoulder a parallel burden of proof. Why don't they have to provide positive grounds in favor of their position rather than simply criticizing the arguments of theists?

To understand this asymmetry of epistemic burdens, we must return to Flew's initial definition of 'atheism'. On Flew's definition an atheist is simply one who lacks belief in God, But how does one go about justifying the *not* having of a belief? In point of fact, it seems that one has no responsibility to justify the *not* having of a particular belief unless there is some reason that it *should* be believed. For instance, I have no responsibility to justify my lack of belief in the existence of a giant gaseous planet in orbit around the star Betelgeuse. Neither do I have to justify the fact that I fail to believe that someone living in my town is named, say, Hieronymus Bosch. I have no responsibility to justify my lack of these beliefs because no one has yet given me any reason to suggest that they ought to be believed.

It therefore seems that, given Flew's definitions, theists do have to bear the burden of proof in their debates with atheists. The reason is simply that the having of a belief demands justifying grounds but, in the absence of such grounds, the lack of belief does not.

Such then is the evidentialist challenge: Unless theists can provide adequate evidence for the claim that God exists, atheism wins by default. There are basically two sorts of ways for theists to meet the evidentialist challenge. One is to accept the challenge, i.e., to shoulder the burden of proof and offer evidence that is believed to establish the existence of God. This is the approach taken by Richard Swinburne, and his effort to offer such evidence will be the topic of the next chapter.

The other sort of response is to challenge the challenge, i.e., to argue that theists are under no responsibility to shoulder any special burden of proof. This is the approach taken by Alvin Plantinga, and his response to the evidentialist will be the topic of the remainder of this chapter.

Plantinga construes the evidentialist challenge as the claim that theistic belief is irrational unless reasons, arguments, or evidence can be adduced in support of God's existence. In other words, Plantinga sees his atheist opponent as being committed to both of the following claims:

(1) "It is irrational or unreasonable to accept theistic belief in the absence of sufficient evidence or reasons."[18]

(2) We have no evidence, or at any rate not sufficient evidence, for the proposition that God exists.

It is the first claim that Plantinga wishes to challenge. He begins by clarifying the notion of irrationality that he regards as underlying the evidentialist challenge:

Suppose we begin by asking what the objector means by describing a belief as *irrational*. What is the force of his claim that theistic belief is irrational, and how is it to be understood? The first thing to see is that this objection is rooted in a *normative* view. It lays down conditions that must be met by anyone whose system of beliefs is *rational*, and here 'rational' is to be taken as a normative or evaluative term. According to the objector there is a right way and a wrong way with respect to belief. People have responsibilities, duties and obligations with respect to their believings just as with respect to ther actions or, if we think believings are a kind of action, their *other* actions.[19]

Plantinga has hit upon a very important point. To accuse people of irrationality is to charge them with *moral* as well as intellectual failure. This, of course, is what makes the charge of irrationality so inflammatory. To accuse someone of irrationality is tantamount to charging that he has sacrificed intellectual integrity. It is a way of saying that someone has formed a belief irresponsibly or dishonestly—through self-deception, say, or perhaps by ignoring easily available contrary evidence. To call someone irrational is to say that he has settled for a belief that he knows, deep down inside, not to be the most reasonable one.

According to Plantinga, therefore, the evidentialist assumes that we have ethical duties concerning what we believe just as we do with respect to how we act. On the basis of such an assumption, it is wrong to cling to a belief we know to be unwarranted, just as it is wrong to persist in an act we know to be unjust. Further, Plantinga sees the evidentialist as charging theists with failure to perform their epistemic duties.[20] According to Plantinga, the evidentialist views belief in God as a dishonest or irresponsible belief— i.e., a belief that people can form only by noncompliance with their epistemic duties (e.g., seeking evidence, attempting to justify the belief, and the like).

Plantinga regards the assumption that we have epistemic duties as plausible:

> There do seem to be duties and obligations with respect to belief, or at any rate in the general *neighborhood* of belief. One's own welfare and that of others sometimes depends on what one believes. If we are descending the Grand Teton and I am setting the anchor for the 120-foot rappel into the Upper Saddle, I have an obligation to form such beliefs as 'this anchor point is solid' only after careful scrutiny and testing. One commissioned to gather intelligence—the spies Joshua sent into Canaan, for example—has an obligation to get it right.[21]

However, says Plantinga, such duties are not absolute, but only prima facie. That is, any such duty can be overridden when, as will sometimes happen, it conflicts with other duties that are more important. For instance, when rappelling down the Grand Teton, I have a responsibility to check my anchor point carefully before concluding that it is solid. However, should a violent electrical storm be approaching rapidly, I also have a duty to set up the rappel quickly. The latter duty might be so urgent as to preclude my checking the anchor point as thoroughly as I should in other circumstances. The duty to check my anchor point carefully is therefore a prima facie duty that can be overridden by a more urgent duty.

Plantinga therefore interprets the evidentialist as claiming that there is a prima facie duty not to believe in God unless adequate evidence, arguments, or reasons can be given for such a belief:

> Perhaps, then, the objector is to be understood as claiming that there is a *prima facie* duty not to believe in God without evidence. This duty can be overridden by circumstances, of course, but there is a *prima facie* obligation to believe propositions of this sort only on the basis of evidence. The theist without evidence, he adds, is flouting this obligation and is therefore not living up to his intellectual obligations.[22]

In short, Plantinga views the evidentialist critique as asserting the following: (*a*) there is a prima facie duty not to believe in God unless that belief can be supported by adequate evidence, arguments, or reasons; (*b*) theists have no contrary duties that override the duty mentioned in (*a*); (*c*) no adequate evidence, arguments, or reasons exist for theistic belief; and, therefore, (*d*) theists are irrational in believing in God.

Before proceeding to Plantinga's reply to the evidentialists, let us pause to ask whether Plantinga has correctly understood the nature of the evidentialist challenge. Do evidentialists wish to assert that belief in God is irrational? Do they charge theists with epistemic malfeasance? Do Hanson, Scriven, or Flew say anything that implies or insinuates such invidious accusations?

Perhaps Scriven can be taken as making such a charge. After all, he does say that "there is no alternative [presumably, no *rational* alternative] to atheism" if the arguments for God's existence fail.[23] Still, there are some indications that Scriven would not condemn *all* theists as irrational. He admits that a six-year-old could rationally believe in Santa Claus. Surely, he would also admit that a fourteen-year-old who was raised in a Christian family and in a Christian community could rationally believe in God simply because that is how he had been taught.

Nevertheless, Scriven's tone does seem rather censorious. Hanson, on the other hand, is at some pains to deny that he wishes to impugn the rationality of believers. His disclaimer is admirably clear:

> My only objective has been to explore some conceptual and logical credentials of the claim 'God exists' so that I can judge whether, for *me*, this could express a belief that I could ever honestly hold. It has never been any part of my intention to "make Christians' heads roll" or to engage in *ad hominem* dialogue of any kind. Nor have I ever urged a believer to abandon his beliefs! (Although many energetic believers have urged me to abandon mine.) Beliefs are private matters and all of us may believe what we please. . . . My sole aim . . . has been to indicate why pure reason and factual experience have thus far been wholly insufficient to make 'God exists' a creditable belief for *me*.[24]

Hanson therefore makes it plain that his only intention has been to articulate and defend *his* reasons for not believing in God. Indeed, he concludes his essay by emphasizing his desire not to offend theists or imply that their beliefs are irrational:

My objective was to write on what I don't believe, and this I have done as candidly and inoffensively as possible. Yet some of you readers are certain to have been offended—experience has taught me that. But *why* are you offended? Why should *my* expression of my views and my reasons for holding them be construed by you as an attack? . . . Perhaps it is because we assume that, in this issue, there is but one right answer—all others being hopelessly wrong. That being presupposed, it follows that my articulation of views which constitute the right answer for me indirectly reflect on all orthodox religious positions as being wrong, antediluvian, illogical, [or] unthinking. . . . Please let me disclaim responsibility for any such reaction on your part. . . . We must all make our own way through this vale of tears, alone and standing on our own two feet. 1 am prepared to stand on principles such as I have articulated here, and am prepared to pay the loser's forfeit if I've erred. But I grant that others may choose their stand in quite a different way.[25]

Hanson therefore explicitly states that he does not wish to be construed as regarding religious orthodoxy to be an unthinking or illogical position. He repeats several times that he is only stating *his* reasons for unbelief, and he freely countenances the possibility of other viewpoints.

Flew specifically addresses the question of whether his presumption of atheism implies that believers are irrational.[26] He anticipates the objection that believers cannot reasonably be expected to begin from a standpoint of unbelief, as the presumption of atheism appears to enjoin. Rather, they must begin from where they are—from the position of belief in God. Once this is granted, the important question is whether, given the coherent, persistent, and compelling nature of religious experiences, the theist is rational in believing in God. Demands for argument and evidence are irrelevant, so the objection goes, because the theist does not *infer* God's existence from the psychological fact that he has certain experiences. Rather, the theist supposedly experiences God in an immediate, noninferential way— much as the visible world is experienced through the sense of sight.

An example might help to clarify what is meant by knowing something on noninferential grounds. When I see a tree, I don't have to convince myself with arguments and evidence that a tree is in the vicinity; I simply see that it is there. When I have the experience I call "seeing a tree," my knowledge that a tree is present is immediate, direct, and not based on any inference. Many religious people claim to have the same sorts of experiences of God. Insofar as that experience is for them as compelling as my experience of a tree is for me, it is surely wrong to say that such persons are irrational in believing in God.

Flew thus seems to dismiss arbitrarily the possibility that there could be noninferential grounds for belief in God. Further, his presumption of atheism seems to imply that belief in God is irrational unless the requisite arguments or evidence can be provided. However, given the coherent, persistent, and compelling nature of the religious believer's experiences, such an implication does not seem justifiable. Surely persons who have such experiences are rationally justified in believing in God, even if they can provide no evidence or arguments in support of such belief.

Flew immediately concedes the important distinction presupposed by the above objection:

> It is one thing to say that a belief is unfounded or well-founded; and quite another to say that it is irrational or rational for some particular person, in his particular time and circumstances, and with his particular experience and lack of experience, to hold or reject that belief. Granted that his usually reliable intelligence were sure that the enemy tank brigade was in the town, it was entirely reasonable for the general also to believe this. But the enemy tanks had in fact pulled back. Yet it was still unexceptionably sensible for the general on his part to refuse to expose his flank to those tanks that were in fact not there.[27]

It therefore seems quite possible for an atheist to regard theism as entirely unfounded (i.e., groundless), yet to concede freely that theism is a rational belief for many people. In other words, atheists can admit without hesitation that religious experience is coherent, persistent, and, for many, compelling. Persons who believe in God on the basis of such experiences can therefore be regarded by atheists as perfectly rational. (Of course, the atheist would deny that the occurrence of such experiences shows theism to be *true*.)

Further, Flew explicitly denies that the presumption of atheism has as its aim

> to require that to be respectable every conviction should first have been reached through the following of an ideally correct procedure.

To insist on the correctness of this presumption as an initial presumption is to make a claim which is itself procedural rather than substantive; and the context for which this particular procedure is being recommended is that of justification rather than of discovery.[28]

In other words, the presumption of atheism does not stipulate an ideal procedure that must be followed in order for a belief to be formed in a rational manner. Neither does such a presumption preclude that knowledge can be grounded noninferentially:

It is useful to be reminded that when we insist that knowledge as opposed to mere belief has to be adequately warranted, this grounding may be a matter either of having sufficient evidence or of being in a position to know directly and without evidence.[29]

It therefore appears that Flew's presumption of atheism neither enjoins theists to start from the standpoint of unbelief nor does it beg any questions about whether God's existence can be known noninferentially.

The presumption of atheism is a procedural recommendation: it is an attempt to establish a framework for the philosophical investigation of the grounds of belief and unbelief. Of course, Flew has opinions about what the *results* of such an investigation will be, viz., that philosophical inquiry will uncover no adequate arguments or evidence for theism.[30] Once again, though, to draw this conclusion does not commit Flew to the claim either that theists have arrived at their position irrationally or that they cannot rationally retain their beliefs on noninferential grounds.

The evidentialist challenge, at least as enunciated by Flew and Hanson, therefore seems to be concerned primarily with the credentials of a *belief* and not with the rationality of *believers*. In other words, Hanson and Flew are interested in making an investigation of the grounds of theistic belief; whether theists are guilty of epistemic misconduct is of little or no concern to them.

What, then, does the evidentialist challenge amount to if it is not to be construed as an attack on the rationality of theistic belief? It is important to remember the context in which the evidentialist challenge is made. For Hanson, the context is one of trying to defend *his* reasons for denying the existence of God. Hanson challenges theists to provide arguments or evidence for God's existence. When, in his view, no such arguments or evidence is forthcoming, he concludes that he is justified in denying the existence of God. This, of course, does not show that theists are irrational in maintaining their beliefs. However, if Hanson's arguments are sound, he does show—what many theists (and agnostics) have denied—that the denial of God's existence is, at least for some people, a perfectly rational and justified belief.

For Flew, the context for which he recommends the presumption of atheism is that of philosophical debate over the question of God's existence.[31] When the *truth* of a proposition is being asserted (as opposed to merely the rationality of believing it), grounds must be offered for regarding that proposition as true. The defense of the claim that God exists is therefore possible only if arguments or evidence can be offered in support of that proposition. The theist, insofar as he wishes to argue that theism is true, must therefore bear a burden of proof.

Recall, however, that the atheist, as that term is defined by Flew, has no corresponding burden of proof. One who lacks a belief is under no obligation to justify that lack unless there is some reason he *should* possess that belief. It follows that if the theist cannot meet the atheist's challenge to provide cogent arguments or evidence for God's existence, the atheist can rightly regard the debate as over and as settled in his favor.

Of course, even if atheists win the debate over God's existence, this does not show that belief in God is irrational. However, it is an important result for the philosophy of religion. Flew's presumption of atheism is therefore invoked to establish the terms of a philosophical debate and not to disparage the rationality of theistic belief. After all, for a belief to be rational, it need not be the kind of belief that can be successfully defended in the context of philosophical debate. For instance, it is surely rational for me to believe in the existence of minds other than my own. However, it is a matter of deep controversy whether the belief in other minds has ever received an adequate *philosophical* justification.

Flew's position is essentially a *defensive* one. Theists frequently are not content with defending the rationality of their own beliefs. Rather, they are often quite aggressive in arguing that others should also hold such beliefs. It is these latter sorts of theists that Flew is primarily addressing. To such persons Flew makes it quite clear that lack of adequate reasons, arguments, or evidence for God's existence is all the justification that unbelief needs. Whether the lack of such reasons, arguments, or evidence makes theism irrational is a different question and one that Flew does not here address.

Plantinga therefore seems to have misconstrued the aim of the evidentialist challenge. He mistakenly sees it as directed at the rationality of believers when, in fact, it is concerned with the grounds for theistic belief. Plantinga thus seems to be in danger of committing the "straw man" fallacy—the fallacy of attributing to your opponent a view that he never in fact espoused, and then proceeding to attack the falsely attributed view rather than his real position.

Plantinga continues his attack by arguing that evidentialism is based upon a bankrupt philosophical framework—what he calls "classical foundationalism" (hereafter referred to simply as "foundationalism").[32] Foundationalists, as the name implies, are those philosophers who seek to establish foundations for knowledge. They begin by noting that certain kinds of beliefs are based on other kinds of beliefs. For instance, my belief that I will graduate could be based upon my belief that I passed all my final examinations. Some beliefs, the foundationalists note, seem to be capable of standing on their own without being based on any others. For instance, I believe that $1 + 1 = 2$ because it just seems self-evident; I don't have to base that belief on any other belief or set of beliefs. Beliefs that can stand on their own in this way (i.e., without being based on another belief or set of beliefs) are called "basic" beliefs.

Foundationalists hold that not just any sort of belief can be a basic belief. Indeed, they hold that most types of beliefs should only be held if they can be based in the right way on other beliefs. For instance, beliefs about who will win the next presidential election cannot be basic (unless we believe in clairvoyance—in which case such a belief would presumably be basic for the clairvoyant). To be reasonable, such beliefs must be based upon a careful weighing and analysis of such data as public opinion, the candidates' respective stands on important issues, media image, and the like.

Foundationalists therefore attempt to identify those types of beliefs that can reasonably be accepted as basic (*properly* basic beliefs, that is), and to make those properly basic beliefs the foundations of all knowledge. Properly basic beliefs are to serve as the foundations for knowledge in the sense that every belief that is not properly basic is to be held only if it is ultimately based on a belief that *is* properly basic. For instance, mathematical truths that are not self-evident, like 2196 × 129 = 283,284 (assuming that there are no mathematical prodigies for whom this is self-evident), cannot be basic beliefs. However, 2196 × 129 = 283,284 can be accepted if it is calculated by a series of steps each of which *is* self-evident (and therefore properly basic).

The same holds for any other belief that is not properly basic. The foundationalist will accept such a nonbasic belief only if arguments or evidence exists that ultimately links that belief back to one that is properly basic. That is, the foundationalist will accept a nonbasic belief only if it is either immediately based on a properly basic belief or if it is part of a chain of nonbasic beliefs, the final link of which is a properly basic belief.

What then are the conditions that, according to the foundationalists, a belief must meet in order to be properly basic?[33] Foundationalists regard a belief as properly basic only if it meets one of the following three conditions: (*a*) it is self-evident, (*b*) it is evident to the senses, or (*c*) it is incorrigible. Each of these conditions, especially the last, requires some explanation.

To say that a proposition is self-evident is to say that it is seen to be true as soon as it is understood. The basic truths of arithmetic and logic are self-evident in this way. As soon as one comes to understand what the symbols '1', '+', '=', and '2' stand for, one will immediately see that '1 + 1 = 2' is true. Likewise, the sentence 'Nobody is both married and unmarried' is seen to be true as soon as its meaning is understood. Of course, self-evidence has to be relativized to each individual person; as we hinted earlier, 2196 × 129 = 283,284 might be self-evident to some mathematical genius.

To say that a proposition is evident to the senses means that it is one that an immediate sense perception reveals to be true. The proposition 'A robin is in the yard' is evident to the senses if I believe it because I am observing a robin in the yard.

Some foundationalists do not think that propositions like 'A robin is in the yard' should count as properly basic. After all, they argue, I could be hallucinating or in some other way deceived when I think I see a robin in the yard. These more cautious foundationalists would count as properly basic only those propositions that are self-evident or those that are called 'incorrigible'.

An incorrigible proposition, though it is not necessarily self-evident, is one that I cannot be wrong about. It is a proposition that must be true if I believe it is true, and false if I believe it false. For instance, though I could be wrong when I assert "A robin is in the yard," I cannot be wrong when I say "It *seems* to me that a robin is in the yard." I cannot possibly be wrong about what *seems* to me to be the case. Statements about what seems to me to be the case can therefore constitute incorrigible propositions *for me.*

Lumping all foundationalists together, the less cautious with the more cautious, we can follow Plantinga in recognizing the following as the fundamental principle of foundationalism:

> A proposition *p* is properly basic for a person S if and only if *p* is either self-evident to S or incorrigible for S or evident to the senses for S.[34]

Let us call the above the "foundationalist principle" (FP for short). Two claims are being made by FP. The first is that a proposition is to be accepted as a properly basic belief *if* it meets the specified conditions. The second claim is that a proposition may be accepted as properly basic *only if* it meets the given conditions.

Plantinga has no quarrel with the first claim.[35] He freely admits that if a proposition is, say, self-evident to someone, then that person should accept that proposition as a basic belief. However, he rejects the second claim as unduly restrictive. Why, he asks, should *only* those beliefs that are self-evident, evident to the senses, or incorrigible be allowed to count as basic? Couldn't a perfectly rational person accept as basic a belief that met none of those conditions? For instance, could not a perfectly rational person accept the existence of God as a basic belief even though God's existence is neither self-evident, nor evident to the senses, nor incorrigible?

It is precisely here, Plantinga claims, that foundationalism provides the basis for the evidentialist objection to theism:

> According to the foundationalist some propositions are properly basic and some are not; those that are not are rationally accepted only on the basis of *evidence,* where evidence must trace back, ultimately, to what *is* properly basic. The existence of God, furthermore, is not among those propositions that are properly basic; hence a person is rational in accepting theistic belief only if he has evidence for it.[36]

In short, foundationalists regard only two sorts of beliefs as rationally acceptable: (a) properly basic beliefs, where the conditions for proper basicality are spelled out in FP, and (b) beliefs that are supported by argument or evidence that ultimately links those beliefs back to other beliefs that *are* properly basic. These conditions are taken as imposing obligations upon what people ought to believe. Anyone who defies these obligations is therefore regarded as irrational by the foundationalists.

Evidentialism, according to Plantinga, is based on the above foundationalist claims.[37] Evidentialists argue that God's existence is not self-evident, evident to the senses, or incorrigible. Therefore, they contend that God's existence cannot be a properly basic belief. Further, they argue that no argument or evidence exists that can link belief in God back to beliefs that are properly basic. Thus, claims Plantinga, the evidentialists appeal to foundationalism to justify their charge that belief in God is irrational.

If the evidentialist objection is indeed based on foundationalism, the collapse of the latter will spell doom for the former. Plantinga therefore directs his fire at foundationalism. First, he notes that FP would deny properly basic status to many beliefs that it seems quite natural to regard as properly basic. For instance, my belief that I had lunch a few hours ago seems to be a properly basic belief even though it is not self-evident, evident to the senses, or incorrigible.

Second, and more important, foundationalism seems to be self-defeating.[38] Why, Plantinga asks, should anyone believe that the only properly basic beliefs are those that are self-evident, evident to the senses, or incorrigible? In other words, why should anyone believe FP itself?

Perhaps someone would claim that FP itself is a properly basic belief. However, this cannot be so since FP is not self-evident, evident to the senses, or incorrigible. In other words, since the principle 'Accept as properly basic only those beliefs that are self-evident, evident to the senses, or incorrigible' is *itself* not self-evident, evident to the senses, or incorrigible, to accept it as a basic belief would be to violate that very principle. To accept FP as a basic belief would therefore violate FP! Surely there must be something wrong if a principle can be accepted only by violating that very principle!

It looks, therefore, as though FP cannot be a properly basic belief. This means that the foundationalist can only rationally believe

FP if arguments or evidence can be given that ultimately base FP on beliefs that are properly basic. However, says Plantinga, no foundationalist has ever succeeded in giving such arguments or evidence.

It appears, he concludes, that foundationalists are forbidden from accepting their own principle. The foundationalist principle is not properly basic and it cannot be supported by arguments or evidence that ultimately base it on beliefs that are properly basic. Therefore, foundationalists cannot rationally accept FP. Foundationalism thus appears to be an entirely self-defeating enterprise: It rests upon principles that can be accepted only by violating those very principles.

Has Plantinga succeeded in demolishing foundationalism? Is there no way for a foundationalism to be modified to escape Plantinga's criticisms? Why, indeed, would anyone ever *want* to be a foundationalist?

At the core of foundationalism is the deep intuition that some beliefs just cannot rationally be accepted as basic. Suppose that the dictator of a small country begins to call himself "The Almighty" and insists that all citizens prostrate themselves before him and address him only in the most worshipful tones. Suppose further that he declares his divinity to be a self-evident truth and orders that all doubters be put to death as blasphemers. Surely *something* is seriously wrong with the dictator's claim to divinity; surely *that* cannot be a properly basic belief. The same judgment would seem to hold with respect to such beliefs as 'Killing innocent people for fun is morally permissible' and 'I can fly simply by flapping my arms'. To allow such beliefs to count as properly basic seems tantamount to having no standards of rationality at all.

Unless we are to decide on a purely ad hoc basis which beliefs can and cannot be properly basic, we have to develop general criteria that will do the job. Foundationalism is one effort to provide such criteria. Since the possession of such criteria would be a great boon, perhaps the foundationalists' project should not be abandoned too hastily.

One philosopher attempts to salvage foundationalism by offering criteria for proper basicality that are not self-defeating in the way that FP is. Anthony Kenny recommends that a belief be accepted as properly basic if and only if it is (*a*) self-evident or fundamental; (*b*) evident to the senses or to memory; or (*c*) defensible by argument, inquiry, or performance.[39]

Criterion (c) is the most important change from that offered in FP. Kenny notes that someone might hold a belief in a basic manner yet still be able to defend that belief with arguments or evidence. The example Kenny gives is his belief that there is such a continent as Australia.[40] Kenny claims that belief in the existence of Australia is a properly basic belief for him. He doesn't base that belief on maps or atlases, for he would reject as erroneous any map or atlas of that region that did not show Australia. Similarly, he would reject the testimony of anyone who claimed to have visited the place where Australia should be and to have found nothing but empty ocean. In other words, Kenny's belief that there is such a place as Australia is for him a more firmly held belief than anything that could count as evidence for or against that belief.

Nevertheless, Kenny notes, if he ever did meet someone who was skeptical about the existence of Australia, then he could provide maps, atlases, travel guides, encyclopedias, etc., in support of his belief.[41] Thus, for Kenny belief in Australia is properly basic, but he could give reasons for that belief to someone for whom it was not basic.

The Kennyan foundationalist therefore avoids the self-defeating problems of the classical foundationalist. Kenny's criteria for proper basicality can be held as a properly basic belief. One of those criteria requires that properly basic beliefs be defensible by argument, and, the Kennyan foundationalist maintains, those criteria are defensible by argument. That is, if challenged by an antifoundationalist, the Kennyan foundationalist could give arguments in favor of his criteria. Thus Kenny's criteria satisfy their own requirements rather than violating themselves in the manner of the classical foundationalist criteria.

The evidentialist objector could seize upon Kenny's criteria for proper basicality, charge that belief in God meets none of the criteria, and thereby conclude that theism is irrational. Thus, before Plantinga can bring down the curtain on foundationalism and, consequently, evidentialism, he has to find some way to deal with Kenny's criteria for proper basicality.

To say that theism does not have to conform to foundationalist criteria is not to say that belief in God is groundless or that it stands without need of justification. Hence, Plantinga devotes considerable space to the elaboration of a philosophical framework for the justification of theism.[42] In recognition of his place in the long line of thinkers in the Calvinist tradition, Plantinga calls his position "Calvinist epistemology" (referred to henceforth as CE).

A basic tenet of CE is that belief in God is a properly basic belief. That is, 'God exists' is seen as a belief that can be rationally held even when it is totally unsupported by argument or evidence. Calvinist epistemology regards belief in God as on par with such beliefs as '1 + 1 = 2' or 'Snow is white' or 'I feel thirsty'. Clearly, these latter beliefs can be rationally held without being based on any other beliefs or supported by argument or evidence. Of course, God's existence is not, like those other beliefs, self-evident, evident to the senses, or incorrigible. However, for Plantinga, the foundationalist strictures that would have ruled out theism on that basis have now been eliminated.

Plantinga is aware that an apparent difficulty arises here. If God's existence can be rationally accepted even though it is supported by no argument or evidence, why couldn't just about any belief be accepted in the same way?[43] Why couldn't astrology, say, or voodoo be accepted as properly basic beliefs? The elimination of foundationalism may have gotten rid of unduly harsh restrictions on proper basicality, but now it looks like we might have the opposite problem. Hasn't Plantinga thrown open the floodgates of superstition and irrationality? If we eliminate the foundationalist criteria for proper basicality but have no new standards to put in their place, what is to prevent anyone from claiming just about any sort of belief as properly basic?

Plantinga calls this the "Great Pumpkin" objection because it charges that CE would license nearly any sort of belief as properly basic, even the belief that the Great Pumpkin returns every Halloween. Far from allowing any and every belief to count as properly basic, Plantinga replies, CE recognizes that beliefs can be properly basic in some circumstances but not in others.[44] For instance, my belief that am seeing a tree can be properly basic when I am walking in the woods on a clear day, but not when I am sitting in my living room listening to music with my eyes closed. Further, CE holds that there are certain circumstances in which belief in God's existence is properly basic (the specific circumstances will be examined below), but that there are other circumstances in which that belief may very well not be properly basic.

Why, Plantinga asks, would anyone think that such claims commit the proponent of CE to the view that anything goes? Perhaps underlying that charge is the recognition that Plantinga has eliminated the foundationalist criteria for proper basicality but has offered no better criteria to take their place. In the absence of such criteria, what is to prevent a "Linusian epistemologist" from maintaining that great-pumpkinism is properly basic in certain circumstances?

Plantinga replies that some judgments about proper basicality are possible even in the absence of precise, well-defined criteria.[45] Consider an analogy: Surely "The slithy toves did gyre and gymble in the wabe" can be judged meaningless even if we do not possess absolutely general criteria that would unambiguously settle every question about meaning. That is, we can know that sentences like 'Colorless green ideas sleep furiously' are meaningingless even if we can't say exactly why. Likewise, Plantinga asserts, certain beliefs can be judged properly basic and others not even in the absence of criteria for proper basicality. Thus, I don't seem to need any explicit criteria to judge justifiably that '1 + 1 = 2' is properly basic but that 'The Great Pumpkin will return next Halloween' is not.

However, Plantinga does recognize that criteria for proper basicality would be good and useful things to have.[46] There are bound to be many borderline cases in which certain beliefs are neither obviously properly basic nor obviously not properly basic. Such criteria would allow us to determine the category to which these borderline cases really belong.

Indeed, since all of our beliefs are either basic or ultimately based on basic beliefs, our criteria for proper basicality will in large measure determine what it is rational for us to believe. Remember that rationality is defined by rules that tell us what we ought and ought not to believe. Perhaps the most important set of such rules is our criteria for proper basicality.

Plantinga thinks that the way to develop such criteria is by following an *inductive* procedure:

> We must assemble examples of beliefs and conditions such that the former are obviously properly basic in the latter, and examples of beliefs and conditions such that the former are obviously *not* properly basic in the latter. We must then frame hypotheses as to the necessary and sufficient conditions of proper basicality and test these hypotheses by reference to those examples.[47]

In other words, we begin by taking note of those beliefs that we hold to be *obviously* properly basic and those that we hold to be equally obviously *not* properly basic. We then closely analyze the precise circumstances in which we either accept or reject those beliefs as properly basic. On the basis of that analysis we can begin to formulate hypotheses about what types of beliefs are to count as properly basic in what sorts of circumstances.

For instance, I might accept the belief 'My stomach is empty' as obviously properly basic whenever I am in the circumstance of experiencing certain characteristic abdominal pangs. On the other hand, I might note that I do not accept 'My stomach is empty' as properly basic whenever I happen to notice that it is an hour after my usual time for taking lunch. I might have had an unusually large breakfast so that my stomach is not empty by my usual lunch time. From a large number of such examples I might eventually formulate the following criterion: "Accept beliefs about your internal bodily states as properly basic only when you experience certain characteristic feelings."

Once such criteria have been formulated, they can be tested against concrete cases. That is, such criteria will be confirmed if each time we discover a new, obviously properly basic belief it conforms to those criteria. For instance, the above criterion is confirmed if, after formulating it, I notice that I accept beliefs about my heart rate as properly basic only when I feel my pulse thumping in a characteristic way.

On the other hand, such criteria would be disconfirmed if an instance of obvious proper basicality were found to run against them. For instance, a doctor might discover that she is pregnant by performing an ultrasound test on herself. She makes this discovery by looking at an image on a screen rather than by having a characteristic feeling. Nevertheless, her belief that she is pregnant seems to be a basic belief; she just *sees* the developing embryo (seeing with an instrument is a form of seeing). Further, that belief seems to be properly basic. We have, therefore, an apparent counterexample to the criterion that beliefs about internal bodily states are properly basic only when certain characteristic feelings are experienced.

By such a process of hypothesis formation and testing, Plantinga believes that adequate sets of criteria can eventually be formulated. Further, he sees no reason to suggest that such criteria would have to permit greatpumpkinism as properly basic just because they allow theism to have that status.

How, then, can theists be sure of having criteria that permit them to regard belief in God as properly basic? Simply by making belief in God one of their examples of obvious proper basicality.[48] That is, if we regard the existence of God as *obviously* properly basic in given circumstances, then the criteria we eventually formulate will, of course, reflect that initial assessment. In other words, since our criteria in large part will derive from what we initially take as obviously properly basic, those criteria will naturally permit the taking of such beliefs as properly basic!

This may strike the reader as a case of pulling oneself up by one's own bootstraps, but it is a perfectly legitimate procedure. The statement '1 + 1 = 2' is obviously a properly basic belief. It therefore constitutes one of the paradigms of proper basicality from which I will endeavor to formulate my criteria. Those criteria, when finally produced, will therefore permit '1 + 1 = 2' to be properly basic.

What, then, are the circumstances in which Plantinga regards belief in God as obviously properly basic? He gives a number of such circumstances:

> Upon reading the Bible, one may be impressed with a deep sense that God is speaking to him. Upon having done what I know is cheap, or wrong, or wicked, I may feel guilty in God's sight and form the belief 'God disapproves of what I have done'. Upon confession and repentance I may feel forgiven, forming the belief 'God forgives me for what I have done'. A person in grave danger may turn to God asking for his protection and help; and of course he or she then has the belief that God is indeed able to hear and help if He sees fit. When life is sweet and satisfying, a spontaneous sense of gratitude may well up within the soul; someone in this condition may thank and praise the Lord for His goodness, and will of course have the accompanying belief that indeed the Lord is to be thanked and praised.[49]

Plantinga claims that it is clearly rational for persons in such circumstances to form a spontaneous belief in God. Here belief in God arises naturally—just as the belief that a robin is nearby is formed when I see one bobbing along the sidewalk in front of me. My belief that a robin is nearby, in the circumstance just mentioned, is not formed by a process of argument or inferred from evidence. I know that the robin is there because I see it. Likewise, Plantinga claims, I can know that God exists when, for instance, I hear Him speaking to me through the Bible or come under the conviction of my own sinfulness and need for redemption. Such circumstances constitute the grounds for belief in God just as instances of seeing robins are the grounds for belief in robins. Belief in God in the above circumstances is therefore, says Plantinga, an obviously properly basic belief.

Plantinga's defense of the rationality of theism is thus essentially complete. The evidentialist objection is construed as holding theism to be irrational unless it is supported by argument or evidence. Plantinga has further argued that evidentialism is based upon classical foundationalism, and has shown that classical foundationalism is self-defeating because it cannot be accepted without violating its own standards. In addition, Plantinga has argued that belief in God is properly basic and can therefore be rationally accepted even though it is supported by no argument or evidence. He anticipates the objection that by allowing belief in God to count as properly basic, the door is open for just about any belief to be granted that status. Plantinga rebuts that charge and shows how the theist can develop criteria for proper basicality. Plantinga thus regards the evidentialist objection as defeated and the rationality of belief in God as fully vindicated.

What are we to make of Plantinga's argument? Has he overcome the evidentialist challenge? Has he shown that theism is a rational belief? We have seen that there is good reason to question whether the rationality of theism is the main issue raised by the evidentialists. However, let us suppose that it is. That is, let us suppose that the evidentialist challenge means to assert that theism is irrational unless it is supported by argument or evidence. Has Plantinga adequately answered such a challenge?

Let us first return to the "Great Pumpkin" objection. Recall that Plantinga anticipates this objection: if the existence of God is to be allowed as properly basic, then it would seem that just about any other sort of belief would have to be so allowed. Surely, if CE thus legitimized almost any sort of superstition or irrationality, it would constitute no improvement over foundationalism. To allow just anything to count as rational is to have no rationality at all. Indeed, rather than accept such an alternative, it would seem vastly preferable to try to salvage something from the foundationalist project. At least the foundationalist criteria have the virtue of eliminating much patent nonsense.

Plantinga's reply to the "Great Pumpkin" objection was, first, that not all judgments about proper basicality need to be grounded in criteria, and, second, that CE allows for the inductive formulation of such criteria. These replies certainly show that Plantinga himself is not required to accept, say, astrology or voodoo as properly basic. But is this the issue? Is the important question whether or not CE would allow *Plantinga* to hold these things as properly basic? Perhaps the crucial issue is whether CE provides any grounds for denying that *others* have the right to make such claims. After all, what would Plantinga say to a Shirley MacLaine who claims to recall her past lives, or to a Jeane Dixon who claims to receive guidance from the stars, or, indeed, to a Linus Van Pelt who is sure that his pumpkin patch is the most sincere and will be visited by the Great Pumpkin this Halloween? Can CE be acceptable if it allows such claims?

Perhaps Plantinga would reply that it is not his concern to make judgments about other people's rationality. Perhaps he is only concerned to show that the fact that someone accepts the existence of God as properly basic doesn't mean that *that* person is thereby committed to accepting practically any belief as properly basic. Maybe we can speak for ourselves, but we cannot impose standards of proper basicality on the MacLaines, Dixons, and Van Pelts of the world.

That we are thus forbidden from imposing our criteria for proper basicality on others seems to follow from the way that such criteria are formulated in CE. According to CE, we should begin our formulation of criteria for proper basicality by noting which beliefs seem obviously properly basic *to us* and which do not. However, if *anything* is obvious, it is that what seems obvious to one person might not seem the least bit obvious to someone else. Therefore, it should not be surprising if different people regard different sets of beliefs as obviously properly basic. For instance, when walking in the desert I might regard it as obvious that a good-sized pool of water is located in the middle distance. However, one who has superior knowledge of desert mirages might not regard this as obvious.

Since different people regard different beliefs as obvious, it is not to be expected that the inductive formulation of criteria—the procedure recommended by CE—will result in the same set of criteria for everybody. If two people start with fundamentally different paradigms of proper basicality, then the rules that they construct on those paradigms will also be quite different. They may even be incompatible. However, since a person's rules derive from *his* paradigms, he can hardly expect his rules to apply to someone who starts with a fundamentally different set of examples. This seems to imply that a belief might be rationally accepted as basic by one person but equally rationally rejected by another. Again, it all depends on which set of beliefs is initially taken as obviously properly basic.

Further, it does not seem to be possible to settle such disagreements by argument. Criteria for proper basicality, in the context of CE, can only be justified by an appeal to the examples from which they derived. When the examples themselves are incompatibly different, there remains no common ground upon which disagreements over criteria can be settled. Of course, if a person's beliefs are inconsistent with his *own* criteria—as Plantinga argued the classical foundationalist's beliefs to be—then irrationality can be charged. However, unless someone's beliefs are inconsistent, incoherent, or self-refuting, there seems to be no way to show that they are irrational in accepting as properly basic whatever they happen to accept.

Plantinga thus appears to side with the many philosophers who see the death of foundationalism as spelling the end of the long search for a single, transcendent touchstone for rationality.[50] The history of Western philosophy is in large measure the story of the search for some single set of criteria that would settle, once and for all, which beliefs can be rationally held and which cannot.

The abandonment of that search seems to entail that no one philosophy, perspective, ideology, conceptual scheme, or world view can make absolute claims for itself. Each must be considered rational within its own sphere. In the antifoundationalist's garden, thousands of flowers are allowed to bloom. Indeed, one prominent antifoundationalist sees the collapse of foundationalism as finally allowing all the voices to be heard in the "conversation of mankind."[51] Hopi myths and African folk tales can be listened to as respectfully as particle physics since there is no objective criterion to suggest that it is more rational to believe the latter than the former.

Indeed, it would appear that for the antifoundationalist all judgments about rationality are context dependent in that they can only be deployed *within* a given conceptual scheme, world view, etc. If someone starts with a set of basic beliefs fundamentally different from ours, then *our* conception of rationality need not apply to that person. Calvinist epistemology, with its emphasis on the inductive formulation of criteria for proper basicality, seems to fit right in with the antifoundationalist program.

Perhaps the antifoundationalists are right and there is no objective, universal litmus test of rationality. Perhaps the search for such criteria is a will-o'-the-wisp. Indeed, the search for such criteria may be the greatest intellectual boondoggle in human history, having occupied the efforts of many more of humanity's greatest minds than did the search for the philosopher's stone or the elixir of life.

Nevertheless, it is a very strong and persistent illusion—if it be an illusion—that some beliefs are just irrational, even if they are consistent, coherent, and don't fall into any self-referential traps (i.e., they don't stipulate any principles that can be accepted only by violating those very principles). Flat-earthers, Nazis, "scientific" creationists, Moonies, Velikovskyans, Scientologists, Lyndon Larouchians, astrologers, New Agers, and Shi'ite fundamentalists all seem to be capable of expressing their views without contradicting themselves, lapsing into incoherence, or falling into self-referential traps. Indeed, Martin Gardner has recently reported a mathematically sophisticated defense of the view that the earth is hollow and that we live on the *inside!*[52] This "hollow earth" model is mathematically irreproachable and, with appropriate adjustments of the laws of nature, incapable of being falsified empirically!

However, it is hard to shake the gut-level conviction that many such beliefs are simply irrational. It is a very powerful intuition that *some* epistemic duty is being violated by anyone who, say, denies that the Jewish Holocaust ever occurred—even if such a person does not contradict himself, lapse into incoherence, or enunciate principles that could be accepted only by violating those very principles. Given such powerful intuitions, perhaps we should not take Plantinga's quick *reductio ad absurdum* as the last word on foundationalism. Perhaps, instead of rushing headlong into CE or some other brand of antifoundationalism, we should follow Kenny's example and try to refurbish some set of general criteria for rationality.

In short, almost everyone feels that *some* beliefs are just *too* ridiculous to be held by any honest and responsible believer. If CE would sanction such beliefs as properly basic for some persons, it will be hard to settle on it as a basis for the defense of the rationality of theism.

For Plantinga, however, a much more crucial point is this: There is something very odd about a defense of theism that would make it only one of indefinitely many rational belief systems. Historically, theism has sought to challenge opposing beliefs rather than accommodate them. Theists have traditionally asserted that belief in God is rationally *superior* to such alternatives as dualism, deism, polytheism, pantheism, atheism, and agnosticism.

However, given the principles of CE, it appears that theists can no longer claim such superiority. If atheism, for instance, is not inconsistent, incoherent, or self-refuting—and atheists can confidently defy anyone to show that it is any of these things—then it seems that Plantinga must accept it as an equally rational alternative to theism. After all, assuming that atheism meets its *own* criteria, what can he say against it? *His* criteria derive from his own set of examples of obvious proper basicality, and the atheist will clearly start with a fundamentally different set of examples, Whereas the existence of God is obviously properly basic for Plantinga, it is obviously *not* properly basic for the atheist. Indeed, there seems to be no reason, given CE, to prevent the atheist from starting with the *nonexistence* of God as obviously properly basic! Calvinist epistemology thus seems to cut both ways: If it deprives atheists of the charge that theism is irrational, it deprives theists of the same charge against atheists.

At this juncture the atheist might pause to take stock. If Alvin Plantinga, perhaps the leading philosophical defender of theism, concedes that it is completely rational not to believe in God, why push the point any further? Atheists are seldom interested in gaining converts. They don't proselytize on television or visit school yards to distribute copies of the writings of Bertrand Russell. Most atheists would be pleased with a "live and let live" arrangement with theists.

Nearly all of the objections to such an arrangement will come from Plantinga's fellow theists. For instance, Shabbir Akhtar, a Muslim, has recently criticized those who claim no more for theism than that it is rationally on a par with atheism. Akhtar criticizes what he calls the "parity argument":

> Under these circumstances [i.e., when theists claim mere parity with atheists] there is no convincing reason why any atheist or agnostic should come to religious faith nor indeed, more significantly, why a believer should feel morally or religiously obliged to contend indefinitely with doubts he may experience about the authenticity or truth of his convictions. It is not enough that religious practices or experiences

provide sufficient sustenance to reinforce those who are already *within* the circle of faith: religion must provide something that challenges those who are *outside* of it.[53]

As we have seen, Saint Paul would have rejected the idea that theists can claim no more than that belief in God is just as rational as unbelief. Muslims and orthodox Jews would certainly concur. It is an integral part of Roman Catholic doctrine that the existence of God can be demonstrated using the natural powers of reason possessed by all humans. Hence, Catholics can scarcely regard atheism as fully rational. Protestant fundamentalists generally regard the historical arguments for the Resurrection or the authenticity of the Bible as showing the superior rationality of their beliefs. Even John Calvin, whom Plantinga quotes approvingly, regards unbelief as rationally inexcusable. Surely, there is something very odd about a defense of theism that so many atheists would willingly accept and so many theists would vehemently reject.

Indeed, the old-fashioned theists have a point: How can one claim to possess an absolute truth when one holds rationality to be entirely relative? For the theist, the belief that God exists is not merely rational, not merely *a* truth; it is *the* Truth—Truth with a capital "T." How can theists claim that God's existence is the ultimate, absolute Truth and simultaneously concede that atheists are equally rational in not believing that alleged Truth? To say that there are irreconcilably different standards of rationality is to concede that there is no neutral framework, sanctioned by those divergent standards, for the adjudication of conflicting claims. It is to say that when different standards are employed to endorse incompatible beliefs, there is no unbiased, impartial tribunal that can tell us which claim, if either, is in fact objectively true. Indeed, the whole conception of 'objective' truth seems to break down in such circumstances. It appears that if rationality is relative, truth is also.

Again: If I say that I am perfectly rational in believing P and that you are perfectly rational in believing not-P, and no common grounds can be established that would allow us to reconcile our differences, then how can I categorically state that, nevertheless, you are *wrong*? Of course, I have to go with what seems right to me and you have to go with what seems right to you. But Ultimate Truth—if such a concept can be applied at all in such a context— eludes us both.

Those who say that unbelief is just as rational as belief therefore cannot also claim that 'God exists' is true in any nonrelativistic sense. Hence, insofar as Plantinga wants to maintain, as it seems that all theists must, that God's existence is the ultimate, absolute Truth, then he must deny that atheism can be as rational as theism.

Perhaps, then, we have so far misconstrued Plantinga. Perhaps he does want to claim that atheism is irrational, or at least less rational than theism. For the sake of argument, let us assume that he does want to make such a claim. However, it is very hard to see how he can argue this. He offers no arguments or proofs for God's existence. He doesn't show that atheism is in any way inconsistent, incoherent, or self-refuting. The principles of CE seem to preclude that Plantinga could inductively formulate criteria that would tell against atheism. Atheists start from a fundamentally different set of paradigms and so would be under no obligation to accept Plantinga's criteria. In the absence of argument, an atheist would rightly view the charge of irrationality to be as blatant a case of intellectual imperialism as that of which any foundationalist was ever guilty.

Indeed, if atheists are irrational, what epistemic duty are they violating? Theists agree that a belief must be supported by arguments or evidence if it is not properly basic and that if it cannot be so supported it ought not to be believed. Atheists do not regard belief in God as properly basic and they can discover no arguments or evidence for that belief, so in declining to believe in God they are following principles sanctioned by theists.

Given their initial paradigms of proper basicality, atheists therefore seem to be fully rational in not believing in God. Perhaps, then, Plantinga wants to argue that the irrationality of atheism lies in the initial decision of atheists not to count belief in God's existence as an instance of obvious proper basicality.

But again the question arises: What, exactly, is the epistemic duty that atheists are violating here? What rule of rationality have they broken by not taking the existence of God as obviously properly basic? The following rules seem to be the only possible candidates for such alleged duties:

R_1: Accept as obviously properly basic whatever is obviously properly basic to *theists*.

R₂: Accept as obviously properly basic whatever *is* obviously properly basic.

R₃: Accept as obviously properly basic whatever is obviously properly basic to *you*.

R₁ can be rejected right away as a blatant piece of intellectual imperialism. How could I possibly have the duty of accepting something as obvious just because someone else finds it obvious? R₂ can be rejected just as quickly. It presupposes that some neutral framework exists to adjudicate between what I find obvious and what you find obvious. But there is no such neutral framework.

R₃ is certainly a legitimate rule of rationality. Someone would certainly be irrational if something seemed obviously properly basic to that person and was rejected anyway. If Plantinga wants to consider atheists irrational, he must hold that they violate R₃. That is, he must hold that atheists perversely omit belief in the existence of God from their list of obviously properly basic beliefs even though there are circumstances in which God's existence *does* seem obviously properly basic for them. But how can Plantinga know that? It seems we must ask Plantinga the same question we asked Saint Paul at the beginning of this chapter: How can you judge that someone does find something obvious so long as that person consistently speaks and acts as though he does not?

Perhaps there are times when atheists, by word or deed, betray that they do in fact find God's existence to be an obviously properly basic belief. Indeed, there might be times when they betray that, deep down inside, they are convinced of God's existence. In several places Plantinga appears to endorse the Calvinist view that within each human being God has implanted an innate awareness of Himself.[54] It might be argued that there is such an innate tendency and that the only reason that anyone is an atheist is that such a person has allowed sin to eclipse that awareness. Perhaps atheists are irrational in that they refuse to accept as basic a belief that, deep down inside, they know to be true.

Atheists are likely to dismiss such an argument as hopeless question-begging. However, supposing that there is a God and that there is within each human being an innate tendency to acknowledge His existence, is there any reason to think that people will often irrationally deny that innate awareness?

Let us attempt to offer such an argument: Belief in God requires more than mere intellectual assent to his existence. To believe in God is to acknowledge him as Lord, to surrender our lives to him, and to give up our autonomy by conforming our will to his. Further, belief in God carries with it a profound recognition of our own sinfulness and imperfection. This means that the believer must forsake sinful pleasures, not only sinful pleasures of the flesh, but the even more seductive sins of the spirit—such as taking inordinate pride in our own goodness and talents.

For many people, the above conditions will seem intolerable. These persons will want to go on cherishing the illusion that they are in control of their own lives (when, in fact, it is sin that controls them). They have their own plans, goals, and aspirations and do not want God to interfere. They refuse to listen to the quiet, persistent inner voice telling them that their heedless pursuit of worldly pride and pleasure is the pursuit of sham and delusion. Clearly, such persons, in their rebellion against God, will even ignore the inner testimony of their innate spiritual promptings. Indeed, they will resort to any sort of dishonesty or irresponsibility in their thinking so long as that frees them to continue to deny God.

Again, atheists are unlikely to think much of the above argument, but perhaps it need not be addressed to them. Maybe it could be employed by theists to justify their own belief in the irrationality of atheism. Plantinga might therefore claim that a proponent of CE can justifiably claim that atheism is irrational, even if he has no way to make atheists aware of their own purported epistemic misconduct.

Indeed, Plantinga might not need an argument at all. He might simply dig in his heels and declare that the irrationality of atheism is a properly basic belief for him.

However, if Plantinga wants to play hardball, the atheist can do so too by declaring it to be his properly basic belief that anyone who takes the existence of God as properly basic is irrational in doing so. On the other hand, arguments are available to the atheist which support the view that it is theists who are more likely to be irrational. For the sake of fairness, since the theistic arguments for the irrationality of atheism have been given, let us present these: The world is a grim and frightening place; it threatens us constantly with pain, sorrow, and death. Nature obeys her own laws, oblivious of the suffering or hardship they might cause us. Further, even if we do discover happiness, we know that it will be short-lived and that we will die someday. Surely it would be wonderful if, living in such a world, we could be assured that Someone is ultimately in charge—Someone who loves us and will guide and comfort us through life's travails.

Thus does belief in God come about—as a product of hope and fear. Terrified and confused in the face of an indifferent cosmos, people invent God as a comforting father figure, the benevolent patriarch who someday will dry every tear and right every wrong. Thus it seems that belief in God is the projection of the infantile wish to be cradled and comforted by a loving parent who is much wiser and more powerful than we are.

Further, if such wish projection were not enough to keep belief in God going, there are other explanations. Rulers know that an oppressed populace will not so stridently demand justice in the here and now if they can be assured of pie in the sky when they die. Thus, belief in God, with its attendant promises of rewards and punishments (safely postponed to the hereafter), is a powerful tool for social control. Recognizing this, those who govern a society will strongly reinforce the approved religious doctrines.[55]

Atheists can therefore argue that the internal pressure of psychological need and the external pressure of socialization are overwhelming. People succumb to these pressures by believing in God even though the more reasonable alternative of not believing is readily available to them.

Of course, the theist who believes that he has rational grounds for the belief in God will be no more impressed by the above argument than the atheist was impressed by the corresponding theistic argument. However, if the atheist can discover nothing that *he* considers a reasonable basis for belief in God, then he would seem to have every right to hold that theistic belief is the product of irrational surrender to psychological and social pressures. That is, he is well within his epistemic rights in holding that, deep down inside, theists know that their belief in God is groundless but irrationally refuse to give it up. He might not have any arguments that would force theists to admit that their beliefs have an irrational basis, but there seems to be no reason to suggest that he himself could not hold such an opinion. Hence, if it has been any part of Plantinga's project to deny atheists the right to consider theism irrational, then he has clearly failed on that point.

The upshot is that, on Plantinga's principles, if atheists should regard theism as rational, then theists should make the same judgment about atheism. On the other hand, if theists have the right to consider atheism irrational, atheists would seem to have just as much right to say the same about theism. Either way, there is no reason to think that the majority of atheists would be unhappy with such an outcome.

Some theists and most atheists might be happy with such a Mexican standoff, but it seems a disappointing denouement for the philosophy of religion. Are two thousand years of debate to end on such an inconclusive note? Is there no hope that shared criteria for rationality might be hammered out that would at least provide a common framework for debate? Are we each to climb within the protective walls of our own criteria and gaze with insipid tolerance or impotent hostility at those ensconced within different criteria?

At this point Plantinga might remind us that acceptance of CE does not mean an end to all argument between theists and atheists.[56] Each could attempt to formulate arguments that employ only premises that the other would accept. For instance, atheists could argue that central theistic concepts, like that, say, of a bodiless person, are self-contradictory.

But even if atheists are successful in pointing out such contradictions, this does not force theists to give up belief in God. If someone points out that two of your beliefs are inconsistent, it is up to you to decide which one you're going to give up. Hence, whenever it is pointed out to theists that they believe something inconsistent with belief in God, they will simply give up that other belief rather than renounce belief in God. Thus, if it is shown that it is contradictory to suppose that God could both be a person and lack a body, the theist will simply give up the idea of a bodiless person and affirm that God does indeed have some sort of body.

Atheists, of course, can make an exactly parallel move. If they are shown that one of their beliefs implies God's existence, they can simply deny (or at least modify or qualify) that belief and continue to be atheists. Indeed, Plantinga appears to concede that there are no arguments for God's existence that atheists could not rationally deny.[57] Hence, though in theory CE leaves open a door for debate between theists and atheists, in practice that door is shut and padlocked.

There seems to be little prospect for progress in the philosophy of religion so long as each side is content to take refuge in its own criteria of rationality. Theists and atheists can each feel secure in their own domains, but there will be little they can say to challenge the other side. Indeed, the principles of CE, if adopted widely in philosophy, would inevitably lead to the Balkanization of the entire field. That is, philosophy would divide, like the Balkan countries prior to World War I, into many petty states—each sovereign within the narrow confines of its own borders but none having any real power.

Has Plantinga proven theism rational? Well, he seems to have insulated it against being proven *irrational* in certain ways. That is, he has shown that theism cannot be proven irrational by a demand for evidence or an appeal to classical foundationalist criteria. However, to show that theism is not necessarily irrational is not the same thing as proving it rational. The atheist, as we have seen, is still fully justified in regarding theism as irrational.

But perhaps Plantinga has all along been addressing only his fellow theists and does not care a fig what atheists think about the rationality of theism. Has Plantinga succeeded in proving to his fellow theists that they need not worry that the evidentialist objection will prove their belief in God irrational? Well, he certainly seems to have been successful in doing so, though it appears unlikely that many theists needed convincing on that point.

The majority of theists are not likely to find Plantinga's approach very satisfying. Most theists still want to be able to argue that theism is *true* and not merely that atheists cannot prove it false or irrational. Unless atheism can be shown to be inconsistent, incoherent, or self-refuting (and this seems to be a hopeless task), the only way to argue the truth of theism is to establish common ground with atheists. That is, theists must seek to establish *shared* principles of rationality with atheists. This means that they must seek agreement with their adversaries on such things as the canons of argument and evidence and the criteria for proper basicality. Indeed, before two people can meaningfully disagree over the truth of a proposition, they must agree on what it would take to show that proposition true or false.

For the debate between theists and atheists to proceed past the point where Plantinga has left it, someone must therefore be willing to take some risks. That is, someone must be willing to offer arguments for theism that are to be evaluated by criteria held in common with atheists. Of course, this is a bit risky. The arguments might be shown to fail on those criteria and theism will come off looking the worse for it. However, in philosophy as elsewhere the old adage holds: Nothing ventured, nothing gained. The attempt to face these risks by offering such arguments takes us to the next chapter.

NOTES

1. Quoted by Alvin Plantinga in "Reason and Belief in God," in *Faith and Rationality,* ed. Alvin Plantinga and Nicholas Wolterstorff (Notre Dame, Ind.: University of Notre Dame Press, 1983), p. 18.

2. Summarized by Plantinga in "Reason and Belief in God" (hereafter referred to as RBG), pp. 24–34.

3. Norwood Russell Hanson, "What I Don't Believe," in *What I Do Not Believe, and Other Essays,* ed. Stephen Toulmin and Harry Wolf (Dordrecht, Holland: D. Reidel, 1971), pp. 309–331.

4. Ibid., pp. 313–14.

5. Ibid., p. 323.

6. Ibid., p. 309.

7. Ibid., p. 310.

8. See, for instance, J. L. Mackie, "Evil and Omnipotence," in *God and Evil,* ed. Nelson Pike (Englewood Cliffs, N.J.: Prentice-Hall, 1964), pp. 46-60.

9. Hanson, "What I Don't Believe," p. 311.

10. Ibid., pp. 310–11.

11. Ibid., pp. 318–23.

12. Ibid., p. 323.

13. Michael Scriven, *Primary Philosophy* (New York: McGraw-Hill, 1966), pp. 103–104.

14. Ibid., p. 102.

15. Antony Flew, "The Presumption of Atheism," in *God, Freedom, and Immortality* (Buffalo, N.Y.: Prometheus Books, 1984), p. 14.

16. Ibid., p. 22.

17. Ibid.

18. Plantinga, RBG, p. 27 (I have renumbered these propositions).

19. Ibid., p. 30.

20. Ibid., p. 34.

21. Ibid., p. 33.

22. Ibid., p. 34.

23. Scriven, *Primary Philosophy,* p. 102.

24. Hanson, "What I Don't Believe," p. 318.

25. Ibid., p. 330.

26. Flew, "The Presumption of Atheism," pp. 23–26.

27. Ibid., p. 24.

28. Ibid., p. 25.

29. Ibid.

30. See Flew's *God and Philosophy* (London: Hutchinson, 1966), p. 194.

31. Flew, "The Presumption of Atheism," pp. 14–15.

32. Plantinga, RBG, pp. 47–63.

33. Ibid., pp. 55–59.

34. Ibid., p. 59.

35. Ibid.

36. Ibid., p. 48.

37. Ibid.

38. Ibid., pp. 59–63.

39. Anthony Kenny, *Faith and Reason* (New York: Columbia University Press, 1983), p. 27.

40. Ibid., p. 18.

41. Ibid., p. 35.

42. Plantinga, RBG, pp. 73–87.

43. Ibid., pp. 74–78.

44. Ibid., pp. 76–78.

45. Ibid., p. 75.

46. Ibid., p. 76.

47. Ibid.

48. Ibid., p. 77.

49. Ibid., p. 80.

50. The best-known recent critique of foundationalism is probably Richard Rorty's *Philosophy and the Mirror of Nature* (Princeton, N.J.: Princeton University Press, 1979).

51. Ibid., pp. 389–94.

52. Martin Gardner, "Occam's Razor and the Nutshell Earth," in the *Skeptical Inquirer* 12, no. 4 (Summer 1988): 355–58.

53. Shabbir Akhtar, *Reason and the Radical Crisis of Faith* (New York: Peter Lang, 1987), p. 197.

54. See Plantinga, RBG, pp. 65–68.

55. These arguments are, of course, the standard Freudian and Marxist explanations of theistic belief. The atheist certainly seems to be within his epistemic rights in accepting such explanations of theistic belief. If so, then the atheist is also justified in holding that the theist is likely to be less than ideally rational in forming beliefs about God. After all, persons in the grip of overpowering social or psychological pressures to believe p are notoriously unlikely to evaluate p according to the same standards of rationality they apply to other beliefs.

56. See Plantinga, RBG, pp. 82–87.

57. See, for instance, Plantinga's statement about the aims of his version of the ontological argument in *Alvin Plantinga,* ed. James E. Tomberlin and Peter van Inwagen (Dordrecht, Holland: D. Reidel, 1985), pp. 383–84.

2

Swinburne and the
Cosmological Argument

At the end of chapter 1 the conclusion was reached that if theistic belief is to be made credible to atheists, theists must agree to cooperate in hammering out shared conceptions of rationality. If this process had to start from scratch, there would not be much hope for the philosophy of religion. Fortunately, though, much common ground already exists. Indeed, since philosophers (or at least those in the analytic tradition) share much the same background, education, language, and, in general, participate in a common intellectual milieu, it would be surprising if they did not share many of the same intuitions about rationality.

One of the deepest and most widely shared convictions about rationality is that the methods and practices of the natural sciences constitute a paradigm of reasoned inquiry. Respect for the natural sciences as a model of objectivity and progress in the acquisition of knowledge is still very widespread—if not quite as universal as it once was. Hence, a belief commands much respect if it legitimately claims to be supported by the canons and methods of scientific inquiry. The proliferation of pseudoscientific doctrines and practices shows how strongly people covet the "scientific" label for their own beliefs.

It comes as no surprise that theistic philosophers have often attempted to support theism with arguments at least similar to the ones employed in the natural sciences. If it could be shown that belief in God is supported by the same types of methods, logic, and evidence that undergird the best scientific theories, this should give the quietus to atheists (who are usually vociferous in their support of science).

Unfortunately for theists, the road toward scientific theism has proven a bumpy one. Attempts to justify theism in this manner often succeed only in making a mockery of scientific reasoning. The pre- posterously misnamed doctrine of "scientific creationism" is the latest of such distortions.[1]

Equally notorious have been the many "God of the gaps" argu- ments. These arguments place God in the ever-shrinking gaps in the domain of the scientifically explicable. Thus, if there are domains that science has yet to explain adequately, such as the functioning of mind or the origin of life, gap-apologists gleefully point to these lacunae and proclaim that only God can account for such mysteries. But, of course, as science inexorably progresses and the gaps are narrowed or closed, defenders of gap arguments must beat a hasty and undignified retreat and begin the search for new gaps.

Even the most sophisticated attempts to provide broadly scientific support for theism have been sharply criticized. David Hume's *Dia- logues Concerning Natural Religion,* published over two centuries ago, remains the classic critique of arguments that seek to place theism on something like a scientific basis.[2] Indeed, Hume's arguments against the "religious hypothesis" were so powerful that many have regarded them as pretty much the final word on the subject.

Nevertheless, the "religious hypothesis" does not lack capable de- fenders in the present day. Richard Swinburne, in his book *The Exis- tence of God,* presents what is easily the most careful, comprehensive, and plausible set of arguments yet offered in defense of theism as an explanatory hypothesis.[3] That is, Swinburne maintains that theism should be treated as a hypothesis that explains why the universe exists and why it possesses its characteristic features. In other words, just as science explains phenomena with hypotheses about atoms, genes, forces, and the like, so, Swinburne believes, other puzzling phenomena can be explained by hypotheses referring to God. Swinburne believes that such a construal will allow theism to be confirmed by evidence in much the same way that evidence supports good scientific hypotheses.

Swinburne examines six arguments supporting and one against theism construed as an explanatory hypothesis. The one antitheistic argument he considers, the argument from evil, will be the subject of the next chapter. Further, one of the theistic arguments he discusses, the argument from morality, is not considered a good argument by Swinburne. The remaining five arguments are treated extensively, far too extensively to be dealt with adequately in this book. Here we will only have room to make a thorough examination of one argument, namely, Swinburne's version of the so-called "cosmological" argument.

Traditionally, cosmological arguments have relied upon the Principle of Sufficient Reason (PSR): that nothing exists unless there is a sufficient reason that explains why it is so and not otherwise.[4] This principle has been taken as intuitively obvious, i.e., as self-evidently true. Indeed, it seems quite plausible. You and I, for instance, would never have existed if many factors had not come together to bring about our births. Our parents' births, the fact that they happened to meet, their decisions to marry and have children, the fact that one particular paternal sperm cell happened to fertilize that one particular maternal ovum, are all factors that led to our existence. If one of those factors had been different—if, for instance, our parents had married different persons—then we would never have existed. When taken together these factors do constitute the sufficient reason for our own existence. When all these factors are put together, they explain why our parents had *us* instead of different children or, perhaps, no children at all.

According to traditional versions of the cosmological argument, PSR applies not just to us but to everything in the universe. That is, everything in the universe is such that it might have been different or might not have existed at all. Further, so the argument goes, since everything in the universe might have been different or might have never existed at all, the same holds true of the universe taken as a whole. Hence, there must be some sufficient reason to explain why the universe exists and why it possesses its particular characteristics. Thus, there must be a sufficient reason that explains why something exists rather than nothing and why what exists is *this* universe and not some other.

Further, the argument goes, we cannot account for the present state of the universe by positing an infinite number of past states of the universe, each state having the previous state as its sufficient reason. In this case the series of states would itself be unexplained. That is, each state might explain why the following state existed, but the series of states taken as a whole would lack explanation. It could still be asked why any series of states exists at all or why *this* series exists and not some other.

To state the sufficient reason for the existence of the universe, it therefore seems that we shall have to look beyond the universe. However, supposing that we do find something beyond the universe that can serve as the sufficient reason for the universe's existence, we would not have gained much if we immediately had to ask after the sufficient reason for *its* existence. Thus, a truly adequate sufficient reason for the universe's existence will have to be something that is beyond the universe and has within itself its own sufficient reason for existing. Such an entity would account for the universe's existence and would need nothing beyond itself to account for its own existence. The cosmological argument holds that only God could be that entity. Only God can be his own sufficient reason and the sufficient reason for the existence of everything else. Thus, the argument concludes, we know that God exists.

The traditional cosmological argument has been subjected to devastating criticism. Getting right to the heart of the matter, many critics have seen PSR as demonstrably false, or at least as wholly unjustified. Thus J. L. Mackie:

> The principle of sufficient reason expresses a demand that things should be intelligible *through and through.* The simple reply to the argument which relies on it is that there is nothing that justifies this demand, and nothing that supports the belief that it is satisfiable even in principle.[5]

That is, PSR regards *nothing* as explained until *everything* is explained. On the contrary, it is logically impossible to explain *everything.* In any explanation, whatever is to be explained (the *explanandum*) is accounted for by whatever explains it (the *explanans*). In order for the *explanandum* to be explained by the *explanans,* the latter must, at least for the moment, go unexplained. Of course, we can then take that *explanans* and try to explain it, but to do so we will have to introduce a new *explanans* that will *itself* be unexplained. Thus, however far we go in our chain of explanations, something will always be unexplained. This is a necessary feature of the logic of explanations. However, it in no way indicates that our explanations of things are at all inadequate. If I explain the collapse of a building by saying it was dynamited, this explanation is not the least bit weakened by my not knowing who dynamited it.

Other objectors have argued against the idea that any being could be a sufficient reason for its own existence.[6] To be the sufficient reason for something usually involves bringing it into existence. Clearly, though, nothing can bring itself into existence. Nor can anything be the explanation of itself. If someone asks "Why is A?" and we answer "Because of A," then the question "Why is A?" immediately arises again and we are right back where we started.

Perhaps defenders of PSR mean that God can be his own sufficient reason in the sense that his existence is logically necessary, i.e., that it is self-contradictory to deny his existence. However, this is to rely upon an entirely different argument altogether—the so-called ontological argument. The ontological argument, which attempts to deduce God's real existence from a statement of the formal properties that define the term 'God', is itself a notorious failure.[7] Hence, defenders of cosmological arguments would do well not to rely on the ontological argument.

Perhaps saying that God is his own sufficient reason means only that he is uncreated, indestructible, and is in no way dependent upon other beings. However, if this is all that it means for an entity to be a sufficient reason for itself, then, it would seem that certain *physical* entities (fundamental particles, for instance) could be their own sufficient reasons in that sense. Indeed, there is no a priori reason that the universe itself could not be uncreated, indestructible, and independent. Hence, to say that God is his own sufficient reason is to say something that is either absurd, false, or unimportant.

To his credit, Swinburne does not attempt to revive the traditional version of the cosmological argument. He does not think that the universe must have a sufficient reason for its existence.[8] The universe, he admits, could conceivably be an ultimate, inexplicable, brute fact. Further, he does not conceive of God as possessing a sufficient reason for His own existence. For Swinburne, it is perfectly conceivable that God does not exist; it just so happens that He does.

Swinburne's argument is an *inductive* one; it is *probabilistic* in nature. That is, though he does not believe that God's existence can be deductively demonstrated, he does think it can be shown that God's existence is more probable than not. With respect to the cosmological argument, Swinburne thinks it can be shown that the universe is more likely to have been brought into existence by God than to have existed uncaused.

Swinburne is an expert in the field of inductive logic known as "confirmation theory"—the study of how scientific theories and hypotheses are confirmed.[9] In particular, Swinburne specializes in Bayesian confirmation theory, named after Thomas Bayes, the English mathematician who first derived the mathematical theorem that Bayesians employ in assessing the strengths and weaknesses of hypotheses.

Bayes's theorem is part of the probability calculus, a mathematical tool for calculating complex probabilities from simple ones.[10] For instance, everyone knows that the probability of getting heads on a single toss of a fair coin is $1/2$; this is a simple probability. A formula of the probability calculus tells us how to figure the complex probability of having heads turn up at least once in two tosses of a fair coin. The formula tells us that the probability of getting heads at least once in two tosses of a fair coin is equal to the probability of getting heads on the first toss ($1/2$) plus the probability of getting heads on the second toss ($1/2$) minus the probability of getting heads on both tosses ($1/4$). The resulting figure of $3/4$ tells us that if we repeated a large number of trials in which we tossed a fair coin twice in each trial, the proportion of those trials in which heads turned up at least once would be very close to $3/4$.

The rudiments of the probability calculus can be learned easily. Here all that will be needed is some familiarity with very basic symbols and concepts. The probability calculus measures the probabilities of many different sorts of things. For instance, it applies to events: to state that the probability of an event is $1/2$ is to say that there is a 50 percent chance that the event will occur. It also applies to properties: to say that the probability of an American being overweight is $1/3$ is to say that one-third of all Americans (or one out of every three) have (has) the property of being overweight.

Here we shall be concerned primarily with the probability calculus as it relates to the truth of *statements*. To say that the probability of a statement A is equal to one—$p(A) = 1$ in the symbolism of probability calculus—is to say that that statement is certainly true. Hence 1 is the highest degree of probability that any statement can have. On the other hand, to say that $p(A) = 0$ is to say that A is certainly false, and hence 0 is the lowest probability any statement can have. If $p(A) = 1/2$, A is just as likely to be true as false. If the probability of A is greater than $1/2$, $p(A) > 1/2$, then A is more likely to be true than false. If the probability of A is less than $1/2$—$p(A) < 1/2$—then A is more likely to be false than true.

The only further concept that must be grasped in order to understand Bayes's theorem is the concept of conditional probability. The same statement can have many different probabilities; it all depends on what other statements we take to be true when we are considering the statement in question. For instance, the statement

A: Billy Bob can quote from Goethe's *Faust*

is highly improbable if all we know about Billy Bob is the statement

B: Billy Bob comes from Boondocks County, and 99.9 percent of the people in Boondocks County cannot quote from Goethe's *Faust*.

However, A is much more probable if all we know about Billy Bob is the statement

C: Billy Bob is a German major at Princeton and 98 percent of German majors at Princeton can quote from Goethe's *Faust*.

Hence, the probability of A given B is very low, only one out of a thousand. In symbols, $p(A/B) = .001$. However, the probability of A given C is very high: $p(A/C) = .98$.

When applied in confirmation theory, Bayes's theorem tells us how to determine a conditional probability. It tells us how to determine the probability that a hypothesis will be true given certain evidence and given all of our relevant background knowledge ("background knowledge" refers to everything we think we know that pertains to the truth of the given hypothesis other than the specific evidence at hand). Symbolically, for any hypothesis *h*, body of evidence *e*, and background knowledge *k*, Bayes's theorem tells us the equivalent of $p(h/e \cdot k)$ is equal to ["·" is just the symbol logicians use for "and"]. The formula for Bayes's theorem is

$$p(e/h \cdot k) = \frac{p(e/h \cdot k)}{p(e/k)} \times p(h/k).$$

Bayes's theorem tells us that the probability of a certain hypothesis relative to a piece of evidence plus our background knowledge—$p(h/e \cdot k)$—depends on three factors: (1) $p(e/h \cdot k)$: the probability that the evidence holds given that the hypothesis is true and given our background knowledge; (2) $p(e/k)$: the probability that the evidence holds independently of our hypothesis, i.e., its probability relative only to our background knowledge; and (3) $p(h/k)$: the probability of the hypothesis being true independently of the particular evidence, i.e., the probability of its truth given only our background knowledge.

A stock example may be used to illustrate how Bayes's theorem is employed in the confirmation of hypotheses. Suppose that Colonel Blimp is found murdered and that suspicion falls upon Hives, the butler. Suppose further that Hives's fingerprints are found on the murder weapon. In this case, h is the hypothesis 'Hives is the murderer', e is the statement 'Hives's fingerprints were found on the murder weapon', and k is everything else we know pertaining to the case, The probability that Hives is the murderer, given that his fingerprints were on the murder weapon and given all other relevant information, $p(h/e \cdot k)$, is determined by the three factors mentioned above.

The probability of h given e and k, $p(h/e \cdot k)$, is *increased* (factor 1) to the extent that it is likely that if Hives did indeed murder Colonel Blimp, his fingerprints would be on the murder weapon. The point here is really quite simple. The more likely it is that Hives would have left his fingerprints on the murder weapon if he really did murder Colonel Blimp, then the more likely it is that he really did murder the colonel given that his fingerprints were found on the murder weapon.

On the other hand, if we know that Hives is a very intelligent and cautious man who would certainly have worn gloves if he had committed a murder, then this greatly decreases the probability that Hives's fingerprints would be on the murder weapon if he were the murderer. This in turn decreases the probability that Hives was the murderer given that his fingerprints were found on the murder weapon.

The likelihood that Hives was the murderer is *decreased* (factor 2) to the extent that it is likely that Hives's fingerprints would be on the murder weapon *whether or not* he had killed Colonel Blimp. In other words, if it is likely that Hives's fingerprints would be on the murder weapon even if he did not murder Colonel Blimp, then the presence of his fingerprints on the murder weapon will not be very good evidence that he is the murderer. Suppose, for instance, that the murder weapon was an ornamental dagger that the colonel had picked up when on duty in the Far East. Suppose further that several witnesses had observed the colonel hand the dagger to Hives with instructions to place it in a display case. It would then be quite likely that Hives's fingerprints would be on the murder weapon even if he were not the murderer. Hence, the presence of his fingerprints on the weapon does not constitute good evidence against him.

The probability of our hypothesis given the evidence and background knowledge is *increased* (factor 3) to the extent that it is likely that Hives was the murderer given everything that we know *other* than the fact that his fingerprints were found on the weapon. If, for instance, we discovered that Hives had a strong motive for killing Colonel Blimp, revenge perhaps, this would increase the probability that Hives was the murderer. On the other hand, if our background knowledge included the fact that Hives had an ostensibly flawless alibi at the time of the murder, this would tend to decrease the overall likelihood that he was the murderer.

In Swinburne's application of Bayes's theorem to the cosmological argument, the hypothesis to be confirmed is 'God exists'. The evidence used to support that hypothesis is 'The universe exists'. Since "the universe" means "everything there is (except God)," and this includes all the facts that are known in our background knowledge, nothing is left over to constitute background knowledge except what philosophers call "tautological knowledge."[11] Tautological knowledge is the realm of logically necessary truths, such as the truths of logic and mathematics. Further, the probability of anything given a logically necessary truth is equivalent to the unconditional probability of that thing. Thus, if the probability of rain tomorrow is $1/2$, the probability of rain tomorrow given that it will either rain or not rain is still $1/2$. Hence, when k is tautological knowledge, it can simply be ignored.

When h = 'God exists' and e = 'The universe exists' then $p(h/e \cdot k)$ is the probability that God exists given that the universe exists, and $p(e/h \cdot k)$ is the probability that the universe exists given that God exists. Probabilites $p(h/k)$ and $p(e/k)$ are a little harder to define. They are what are called intrinsic or purely a priori probabilities. The expression $p(h/k)$ defines the probability that h is true (i.e., that 'God exists' is true) given no evidence or factual information whatsoever (since, as we have seen, k includes only tautological knowledge here). The expression p(e/k) defines the same value for the statement 'The universe exists'. But how can there be such purely abstract probabilities? How can we meaningfully assign a probability to such statements when we have no information upon which to assess such probabilities?

Swinburne thinks that there are such intrinsic probabilities. Many other philosophers, including Alvin Plantinga and other distinguished theists, reject the notion that hypotheses can have intrinsic probabilities.[12] In the course of this chapter we shall come to agree with Plantinga on this point, but for the moment Swinburne's claim will simply be accepted.

In the context of Swinburne's argument, p(h/k) is the probability that God exists as the ultimate, uncaused existent—the unexplained brute fact that lies at the end of every chain of explanations. In other words, if we reject the Principle of Sufficient Reason, then either we have to accept an infinite regress of explanations (A explained in terms of B, B in terms of C, C in terms of D, and so on forever), or we have to believe that the chain comes to an end with an ultimate, uncaused *explicans* that explains everything else and is itself inexplicable. The expression p(h/k) defines the intrinsic probability that God is that ultimate *explicans,* while p(e/k), on the other hand, defines the intrinsic probability that the universe itself, or, rather, its most basic and general features, is the ultimate, uncaused, brute fact. The idea that God is the ultimate brute fact is, of course, the hypothesis of theism. That the universe is the ultimate entity is the hypothesis of naturalism.

Swinburne does not think that the cosmological argument taken by itself can establish that it is probable that God exists given that the universe exists.[13] That is, he does not think that the cosmological argument can show that p(h/e · k) > 1/2. His claim is much more modest. All he claims is that the universe is evidence for God's existence. That is, he claims that the existence of the universe provides *some* support for the claim that God exists, but not necessarily enough support to make it more probable than not that God exists. Of course, the cosmological argument is only one of what Swinburne thinks are five good arguments for God's existence. It might be that none of these arguments in isolation makes God's existence more likely than not, but taken together they might make God's existence highly probable.

Swinburne's claim, therefore, is that the existence of the universe confirms God's existence, i.e., that 'The universe exists' makes 'God exists' more likely to be true than it would otherwise be. To say that evidence confirms a hypothesis is to say that the hypothesis is more likely given that evidence than it would be given only background knowledge. Symbolically, for any e, h, and k, e confirms h if and only if $p(h/e \cdot k) > p(h/k)$. With respect to the cosmological argument, this means that the existence of the universe confirms God's existence if and only if the probability of God's existence given that the universe exists is greater than the intrinsic probability of theism.

One consequence of Bayes's theorem is that a hypothesis is confirmed by a piece of evidence if and only if that evidence is more likely to occur if the hypothesis is true than if that hypothesis is false. Symbolically, for any e, h, and k, $p(h/e \cdot k) > p(h/k)$ if and only if $p(e/h \cdot k) > p(e/{\sim}h \cdot k)$ ("$\sim$" is the logical symbol for "not"). This is called the "relevance condition": it specifies that in order for a piece of evidence to support a hypothesis, the truth of that hypothesis must be relevant to the occurrence of the evidence. The relationship between a hypothesis and its evidence is thus a trade-off. For h to be made more probable by e, e must be more probable given the truth of h. The application of the relevance condition to our murder mystery is obvious: The presence of Hives's fingerprints on the murder weapon supports the hypothesis that Hives was the murderer just in case Hives's fingerprints are more likely to be on the weapon if he was the murderer than if he was not.

The relevance condition means that for Swinburne to show that the existence of the universe confirms the hypothesis that God exists, he must show that the universe is more likely to exist if there is a God than if there is not. This is precisely what Swinburne claims to be shown by the cosmological argument.[14]

For Swinburne, a cosmological argument is one that starts from the existence of any finite object.[15] However, since most such arguments have begun with the existence of the entire cosmos, Swinburne restricts his attention to these.

Cosmological arguments begin with evident facts of experience. It is, for instance, unquestionably true that there exists a complex physical universe. In order for there to be an argument from the existence of the universe to the existence of God it must be shown both that the universe somehow requires explanation and that God is the only—or at least the most likely—source of such explanation.

According to Swinburne, there are two ways that the universe could require such explanation. If the universe has existed for a finite time, then, even if all states of the universe since the first are adequately explained in terms of earlier states, the initial state itself will be unexplained. Of course, since he repudiates the Principle of Sufficient Reason, Swinburne sees no incoherence in the notion of an unexplained first state. However, he will later claim that such inexplicability is unacceptable even though it is coherently conceivable.

Further, Swinburne claims that it is a mystery why the universe should remain in existence over time, whether that time is of finite or infinite duration. That is, even if we allow that the universe is infinitely old and that each state of the universe has a complete scientific explanation in terms of earlier states and the laws of nature, it is claimed that series of states and laws taken as a whole will have no explanation. It is this purported mystery that Swinburne holds to provide the strongest reason for invoking the theistic hypothesis.

Many philosophers have rejected Swinburne's claim that a series taken as a whole can be unexplained even if each member of that series is explained. For instance, Swinburne's claim runs head-on into a famous argument of Hume's:

> In . . . a chain . . . or succession of objects, each part is caused by the part which preceded it, and causes that which succeeded it. Where then is the difficulty? But the *whole,* you say, wants a cause. I answer that the uniting of several parts into a whole, like the uniting of several distinct countries into a kingdom, or several distinct members into one body, is performed merely by an arbitrary act of the mind and has no influence on the nature of things. Did I show you the particular causes of each individual in a collection of twenty particles of matter, I should think it very unreasonable should you afterwards ask me what was the cause of the whole twenty. This is sufficiently explained in explaining the cause of the parts.[16]

As another way of expressing Hume's point, if you knew why each member of a group of six Eskimos was standing at a particular street corner in New York City, it would be pointless to inquire further about why the group as a whole was there.[17]

Swinburne opposes this line of argument with a rather brusquely worded counterclaim:

It would be an error to suppose that if the universe is infinitely old, and each state of the universe at each instant of time has a complete explanation in terms of a previous state of the universe and natural laws (and so God is not invoked), that the existence of the universe throughout infinite time has a complete explanation. . . . It has not. . . . It is totally inexplicable.[18]

Swinburne begins his argument against the Humean claim by stating the principle that the cause of a collection of states is any collection of the causes of each state. Hence, if a is caused by a', b by b', and c by c', the cause of the collection a + b + c is a' + b' + c'. For instance, if lamp a lights because switch a' was thrown, lamp b lights because switch b' was thrown, and lamp c lights because switch c' was thrown, then the cause of the lighting of lamps a, b, and c will be the throwing of switches a', b', and c'. So far Hume would be in complete agreement.

However, when we have a collection of states wherein some states are caused by other states in that same collection, this principle must be modified:

A full cause of the occurrence of a collection of states is any collection of (full) causes of each, which are not members of the former collection. Hence if a full cause of a is b, of b is b', of c is d, and of d is d', then a full cause of a + b + c + d is b' + d'. If a full cause of a is b, of b is c, of c is d, and of d is e, then a full cause of a + b + c + d is e.[19]

For instance, suppose Jones is killed by the house collapsing, the house collapses because the dynamite went off, the dynamite went off because the fuse was lit, and the fuse was lit because Smith set a match to it. Then we would say that the cause of the whole chain of events—the lighting of the fuse, the explosion of the dynamite, the collapse of the house, and Jones's death—was Smith's setting a match to the fuse.

Swinburne concludes that:

Insofar as a finite collection of states has a cause, it has its cause outside the set. Hence if the universe is of finite age, and the only causes of its past states are prior past states (i.e., scientific causality alone operates), the set of past states as a whole will have no cause and so no explanation.[20]

Swinburne contends that the same conclusion applies if the universe is infinite in age and the only causes invoked are past states of the universe and the laws of nature. In this case, though each state of the universe might have a complete scientific explanation, the whole series will lack an explanation since there will be no causes of members of the series that are not themselves members of the series. Swinburne concludes:

> In that case the existence of the universe over infinite time will be an inexplicable brute fact. There will be an explanation [in terms of the laws of nature] . . . of why, once existent, it continues to exist. But what will be inexplicable is the nonexistence of a time before which there was no universe.[21]

Further, there are certain permanent features of the universe, such as the amount of energy it contains, that Swinburne views as requiring explanation.[22] Conservation laws tell us, given that the universe *does* contain a given amount of energy, that it will always contain just that amount. However, it is quite conceivable that the universe could all along have contained a different amount of energy. Therefore, the universe lacks an explanation of why it contains just the amount of energy it does and neither more nor less.

Swinburne realizes that in order to show that the universe *requires* explanation it is not enough to show that it *lacks* explanation.[23] The repudiation of the Principle of Sufficient Reason entails that the ultimate, uncaused reality, whatever that might be, will be an inexplicable brute fact. But if there can exist a terminus of explanation for which no further explanation can be given, why cannot that terminus be the fundamental laws and entities of the physical cosmos rather than God?

According to Swinburne, though there is no incoherence or absurdity in supposing the universe to be the ultimate brute fact, it is very unlikely that it will be. That is, $p(e/k)$ is very close to zero. In fact, Swinburne regards the intrinsic probability of naturalism as so low that the notion of the universe as the ultimate brute fact is hardly more acceptable for him than it would be for a defender of the Principle of Sufficient Reason.

Further, Swinburne maintains that it is very unlikely that any being other than God will be the ultimate, uncaused cause of the universe. That is, he argues that all hypotheses postulating a creator other than the God of theism have a very low order of probability.[24]

It will be recalled that what Swinburne is trying to show is that it is more likely that the universe will exist given that God exists than that it will exist given that God does not exist. In our symbolism, he is trying to show that $p(e/h \cdot k) > p(e/\sim h \cdot k)$. Once this is shown, the "relevance condition" mentioned earlier will have been satisfied, and it will be shown that theism is confirmed by the existence of the universe and hence that Swinburne's cosmological argument is sound.

The probability that the universe will exist given that God does not exist, $p(e/\sim h \cdot k)$, is equal to the probability that the universe is uncaused (which is the hypothesis of naturalism) plus the probability that the universe is caused by some entity other than God. Hence, if, as Swinburne claims, these last two probabilities are both exceedingly small, then it follows that the sum of these two probabilities, $p(e/\sim h \cdot k)$, is still very small. If it is thus extremely unlikely that the universe will exist unless God exists, and it is not equally or more unlikely that God exists, then a theistic explanation of the existence of the universe seems to be warranted.

Further, if we have good reason to believe that the probability that the universe will exist given that God exists—$p(e/h \cdot k)$—is not too low, that is, that it is not too unlikely that this universe is the one that God would create, then we can with some confidence assert that it is more likely that the universe will exist given God's existence than that it will exist given that God does not exist. Symbolically, we will then have shown that $p(e/h \cdot k) > p(e/\sim h \cdot k)$. If we are justified in doing this, we will have shown that the theistic hypothesis satisfies the relevance condition and hence that the universe does supply confirming evidence for the existence of God.

Why, though, is it so very unlikely that the universe will be the ultimate, uncaused brute fact? Why is it also so very improbable that the universe has been caused by some entity other than God? The former question will occupy us first.

According to Swinburne, anything so enormously complex as the physical universe cries out for explanation and so itself is not a good candidate for the terminus of all explanation:

A complex physical universe (existing over endless time or beginning to exist at some finite time) is indeed a rather complex thing. We need to look at our universe and meditate about it, and the complexity should be apparent. There are lots and lots of separate chunks of it. The chunks each have a different finite and not very natural volume, shape, mass etc.—consider the vast diversity of the galaxies, stars, and planets, and pebbles on the seashore. Matter is inert and has no powers which it can choose to exert; it does what it *has* to do. There is just a certain finite amount, or at any rate finite density of it, manifested in the particular bits. . . . There is a complexity, particularity, and finitude about the universe which cries out for explanation.[25]

Swinburne justifies his claim that the universe, in virtue of its complexity, is unlikely to be the ultimate brute fact by appealing to confirmation theory. Swinburne defines the complexity and simplicity of hypotheses in terms of the number of entities, the kinds of entities, and the types of relations between entities that they postulate.[26] Hence, a hypothesis that postulates one or a few entities will, other things being equal, be simpler than one that postulates many entities. The same holds for hypotheses that postulate fewer types of entities or less intricate relationships between entities than rival hypotheses. Given such an understanding of simplicity and complexity, the hypothesis that the physical universe is the ultimate, uncaused existent will be a very complex hypothesis indeed.

It is a fundamental tenet of confirmation theory that extremely complex hypotheses have a very low intrinsic probability unless that complexity is counterbalanced by redeeming virtues such as a very high degree of concordance with background theories.[27] Thus, a hypothesis about the evolution of a particular type of organism might be quite complex, but it will still have a high degree of intrinsic probability if it accords very well with the accepted tenets of evolutionary theory.

However, when our hypothesis concerns the postulation of an ultimate, uncaused entity—the final, unexplained *explanans* in terms of which everything else is to be explained—there seems to be nothing left to serve as background (except, of course, tautological knowledge). In other words, if we are seeking the ultimate terms for the explanation of *everything* (except that ultimate term itself), then, by definition, there will be no background entities, and hence no theories about such entities with which those terms must accord.[28]

Since Swinburne regards naturalism as such an ultimate hypothesis, he holds that background knowledge is irrelevant to the assessment of its intrinsic probability.[29] He maintains that simplicity is the only consideration that has much bearing on the intrinsic probability of ultimate hypotheses. Having, he believes, established that naturalism is a very complex hypothesis, he concludes that it has a very low intrinsic probability.

Perhaps, though, some hypotheses other than theism could postulate very simple beings as the creators of the universe. Swinburne replies that, however simple the beings postulated by other hypotheses might be, the God of theism will be much simpler still.

Swinburne contends that theism is an extremely simple hypothesis because it postulates the uncaused existence of a single entity of a very simple kind.[30] Indeed, God is alleged to be the simplest conceivable kind of person. One reason that God is such an extremely simple entity is that his capacities are infinite:

> To start with, theism postulates a God with capacities which are as great as they logically can be. He is infinitely powerful, omnipotent. That there is an omnipotent God is a simpler hypothesis than the hypothesis that there is a God who has such-and-such limited power (e.g., the power to rearrange matter, but not the power to create it). It is simpler in just the way that the hypothesis that some particle has zero mass, or infinite velocity is simpler than the hypothesis that it has a mass of 0.34127 of some unit or a velocity of 301,000 km/sec. A finite limitation cries out for explanation of why there is just that particular limit, in a way that limitlessness does not. . . . There is . . . a neatness about zero and infinity which particular finite numbers lack. Yet a person with zero capacities would not be a person at all. So in postulating a person with infinite capactiy the theist is postulating a person with the simplest kind of capacity possible.[31]

Hence, if Swinburne is right, theism, insofar as it postulates an omnipotent being, is simpler than any alternative hypothesis postulating a limited, finite entity as the creator of the universe.

Another factor cited as enhancing the simplicity of theism is that God's attributes are claimed to fit together in a particularly intimate and natural way. For instance:

> It would seem most consonant with his omnipotence that an omnipotent being have beliefs which amount to knowledge (for without knowledge of what you are doing you can hardly have the power to do any action). The simplest such supposition is to postulate that the omnipotent being is limited in his knowledge, as in his power, only by logic. In that case he would have all the knowledge that it is logically possible that a person have, i.e., he would be omniscient.[32]

Further:

> For a person to act, he has to have intentions. His intentions might
> be determined by factors outside his control. . . . It would, however,
> seem more consonant with his omnipotence for an omnipotent being
> to be entirely uninfluenced in his choice of intentions on which to
> act by factors outside his control, i.e., to be perfectly free. (For an
> omnipotence which you cannot but use in predetermined ways would
> hardly be worth having.)[33]

Similar arguments are made with respect to God's eternity.[34] An even
stronger claim is made with respect to God's perfect goodness. It
is argued that a being with complete knowledge and perfect freedom
will always necessarily choose the good.[35]

It follows that a hypothesis that postulates an omnipotent, unlimited being who fails to possess one or more of omniscience, perfect
freedom, or eternal existence will not be as simple as theism since
these properties are the ones that it is simplest to suppose an omnipotent
being to possess. Further, a hypothesis postulating a being possessing
all these properties and less than perfect goodness is alleged to be
incoherent. It appears, therefore, that whether an alternative hypothesis
postulates a limited or unlimited being, that being will lack the
simplicity of the theistic God.

Swinburne concludes that it is very unlikely that the universe exists
uncaused and also very unlikely that the universe was created by some
being other than God. Indeed, he sees each of these hypotheses as
having such a low order of probability that the sum total of the
probabilities of all such hypotheses is still very close to zero. Thus,
he claims that the probability that the universe will exist given all
the hypotheses other than theism is very close to zero. On the other
hand, Swinburne does not think that the probability that the universe
will exist given that God exists is very high either; there are too many
other universes that God might have decided to create.[36] However,
he does see the probability that our universe would exist given God's
existence as well above zero, and hence well above the sum total of
the probabilities of all the other hypotheses. In other words, he claims
to have met the "relevance condition" by showing that the universe
is much more likely to exist given that God exists than it would be
given that God does not exist—symbolically, he claims to have shown
that $p(e/h \cdot k) > p(e/\sim h \cdot k)$. To have done this is to have shown

that the existence of the universe does confirm God's existence and hence that the cosmological argument is a good argument.

SWINBURNE'S ARGUMENT AND THOSE OF SCIENCE

In making an evaluation of Swinburne's arguments, it will be helpful to begin by stepping back and looking at the nature of his project as a whole. Swinburne unambiguously affirms that his aim in *The Existence of God* is to provide an argument for theism that is in all relevant aspects identical with certain types of scientific arguments:

> The structure of a cumulative case for theism was thus, I claimed [in *The Existence of God*], the same as the structure of a cumulative case for any unobservable entity, such as a quark or a neutrino. Our grounds for believing in its existence are that it is an entity of a simple kind with simple modes of behavior which leads us to expect the more complex phenomena which we find.[37]

Just how similar, though, are Swinburne's theistic arguments to the grounds upon which physicists base their beliefs about quarks, neutrinos, and other unobservable subatomic entities? To judge Swinburne's claim, we must make a brief excursion into the history of science. In 1932 nuclear physicists recognized only three sorts of subatomic particles—protons, neutrons, and electrons. By the early 1960s, however, a veritable zoo of particles had been discovered, including hundreds of nuclear particles called "hadrons." Since, as Swinburne intimates, scientists seek for underlying simplicity, physicists were deeply chagrined to find such a baffling multitude of what they took to be fundamental particles.[38]

Then, in 1964, Murray Gell-Mann showed how the bewildering variety of hadrons could be accounted for by suggesting that they are composite particles, each constituted by a different combination of a small number of pointlike particles that he called "quarks." Gell-Mann's quark hypothesis was regarded as plausible for precisely the reasons mentioned by Swinburne—it provided a simple account that, if true, would explain a confusingly complex batch of phenomena.

However, the story hardly ends here. As physicist Richard Morris observes, so long as experimental evidence of quarks was lacking, their actual existence was held in doubt:

At first, many physicists regarded quarks as nothing more than a useful mathematical fiction that could be used to impose order upon the chaotic world of subnuclear particles. They didn't believe that the quarks corresponded to anything real. When attempts to find free quarks in nature failed, their suspicions were confirmed. The quark, they concluded, was an imaginary particle that made the job of doing physics somewhat easier.[39]

In other words, in the absence of experimental confirmation, the simplicity and explanatory power of Gell-Mann's model only sufficed to establish quarks as convenient fictions, i.e., doing physics was made easier by thinking of hadrons *as if* they were composed of more fundamental particles.

Morris notes that the first experimental evidence for quarks came in 1968:

In that year, an experiment was performed which indicated that protons, at least, seemed to be composite particles. Beams of high-energy electrons were directed at proton targets in order to probe the internal structure of the latter. It was found that the protons seemed to contain pointlike charges. The quark hypothesis had been confirmed.[40]

Another physicist writes:

Free quarks have never been observed. Yet circumstantial evidence for their existence has mounted steadily. One indication of the soundness of the quark model is its success in predicting the outcome of high-energy collisions of an electron and a positron. . . . The case for the reality of quarks is also supported by the variety of energy levels, or masses, at which certain species of hadron, notably the psi and the upsilon particles, can be observed in accelerator experiments.[41]

The above quotations indicate that the cumulative case for the existence of quarks is based on the experimental confirmation and predictive success of the model, not merely on its simplicity and ability to account for previously known data.

Swinburne's cumulative case for theism, on the other hand, rests upon no experimental evidence, nor does it predict any previously unobserved phenomena. His case rests entirely upon the simplicity of the theistic hypothesis and its purported ability to account for data already in our possession. Hence, contrary to Swinburne's claim, his theistic arguments do not strictly parallel those whereby physicists seek to establish the existence of quarks and neutrinos (neutrinos, by the way, have also been experimentally confirmed).[42]

Swinburne anticipates such an objection and argues that with regard to Bayes's theorem: "It is a matter of indifference . . . whether e is observed before or after the formulation of h. All that matters is the relations of probability holding between e and h. And surely the theorem is correct in that respect."[43]

Swinburne argues that to deny this would introduce a highly subjective element into judgments that should be based upon an objective relationship between evidence and hypothesis. Of course, we do *normally* confirm our hypotheses by subjecting them to experimental tests and by determining their predictive success or failure. However, this need is brought about by the *particular* hypothesis and evidence under consideration and is not a generalizable requirement.

Swinburne further supports the above claim by adducing the example of Newton's laws of motion:

> Newton's theory of motion was judged to be highly probable on the evidence available to men of the late seventeenth century, even though it made no immediately testable predictions, other than the predictions which were already made by laws which were already known and which it explained (e.g., Kepler's laws of planetary motion and Galileo's law of fall). Its high probability arose solely from its being a very simple higher-level theory from which those diverse laws are deducible.[44]

If, therefore, scientists do sometimes justifiably accept new hypotheses purely because of their simplicity and ability to account for presently known phenomena, there seems no reason not to accept the theistic hypothesis if it displays those same virtues.

However, there are important disanalogies between Newton's theory of motion and Swinburne's theistic hypothesis, disanalogies that show how far the latter strays from accepted standards of scientific argument. First, though Newton's laws of motion were not immediately tested, they were fully capable of being tested. In fact, they received spectacular confirmation when Edmund Halley correctly deduced from them that the comet, consequently named for him, would reappear in 1758 (Halley's prediction was made in 1705).

Swinburne's theistic hypothesis, on the other hand, not only fails to imply any immediately testable consequences, but he also apparently regards it as untestable in principle. That is, Swinburne never mentions any previously unknown facts that would confirm his hypothesis by their occurrence or disconfirm it by their nonoccurrence. Instead, he develops the above argument to show that theism should not be dismissed despite its inability to generate test implications.

Any scientist who proposed a hypothesis without making clear what previously unknown facts would serve to confirm or disconfirm that hypothesis would have a low status in his profession.[45] Of course, scientists do sometimes accept new hypotheses even when they do not imply any immediately testable predictions, but they also demand that such hypotheses be *capable* of making testable predictions. In fact, such in-principle testability seems to be the hallmark of every genuinely scientific hypothesis. Being able to "predict" only what is already known, on the other hand, is a hallmark of pseudoscience. Many of the most notorious pseudoscientific theories specialize in *post factum* explanations (i.e., explanations of previously known data) but grow strangely silent when asked to specify some heretofore unknown fact that would test the theory.

But why is the testability of all hypotheses insisted upon by the scientific community? Well, the making of testable theories and hypotheses seems to be part of what it *means* to be an empirical science—why call it "empirical" otherwise? Further, it is hard to see how natural science could ever have gotten off the ground if it did not insist on testability. Magical and supernatural accounts often provide very simple *post factum* explanations.

Explanations in terms of demons, poltergeists, mental telepathy, magic, and other such occult entities and paranormal processes frequently possess a greater simplicity, as Swinburne defines the term, than rival scientific explanations. A demon, for instance, is a single entity, it is a spiritual being and hence not composed of parts; it presumably exercises its power over persons and physical objects in some direct and simple way, and it is in all its deeds actuated by a single motivating drive—malevolence. Hence, explanation of a case of psychosis in terms of demon possession seems much simpler than any of the current psychological or neurological explanations. The simplicity and untestability (How could it ever be shown that demons *do not* cause psychoses?) of such hypotheses gives them great obscurantist potential.

Once such untestable hypotheses become entrenched, they can be very difficult to dislodge. Books such as Bertrand Russell's *Religion and Science* tell of the enormous obstacles to scientific progress imposed by supernaturalism.[46] Indeed, if we allow untestable hypotheses to be accepted purely on the basis of their simplicity and ability to provide *post factum* explanations of known data, it is hard to see how science could ever progress. Virtually *any* phenomenon that we currently think possesses an adequate scientific explanation could be explained more simply in nonscientific terms. Occult powers wielded by disembodied agents could be invoked to cover just about any occurrence.

More important than any of the above considerations is the fact that utterly untestable hypotheses are vacuous; they tell us nothing about the world because they are totally lacking in empirical content. As the philosopher of science Carl Hempel put it:

> If a statement or set of statements is not testable at least in principle, in other words, if it has no test implications at all, then it cannot be significantly proposed or entertained as a scientific hypothesis or theory, for no conceivable empirical finding can then accord or conflict with it. In this case, it has no bearing whatever on empirical phenomena, or as we will also say, it lacks empirical import.[47]

In other words, an untestable hypothesis is one that is so formulated that no conceivable observation, experiment, or empirical finding could prove it right or wrong. But if no conceivable facts would serve to confirm or disconfirm a hypothesis, then empirical findings must be irrelevant to that hypothesis; and if the facts are irrelevant to the hypothesis, the hypothesis must be irrelevant to the facts. In other words, because nothing in the world can tell us about the truth of an untestable hypothesis, such hypotheses can tell us nothing about what is true in our world.

A second disanalogy further distances Swinburne's theistic hypothesis from the Newtonian model. Newton's laws of motion, unlike the quark model and the theistic hypothesis, did not achieve greater explanatory power by postulating the existence of previously unknown entities. Newton proposed a set of simple laws that systematically connected a complex set of phenomena previously thought to be disparate and unconnected. Although his laws later led to the discovery of new entities, like Halley's comet, they were initially proposed as *laws,* i.e., as propositions telling us the regular, predictable ways that certain kinds of entities can be expected to behave. The entities those laws applied to—the moon, comets, cannonballs, etc.—were already known. The quark model and the theistic hypothesis, on the other hand, propose that new entities be postulated to account for known ones.

The above suggests that a fundamental distinction needs to be made between two different types of explanatory hypotheses: The first—let us call them L-hypotheses—explain known phenomena by postulating simplifying and unifying laws that govern the behavior of and relations between those phenomena. The second type—call them E-hypotheses—explain known phenomena through the postulation of a new entity or set of entities.

The criterion of simplicity relates to these two types of hypotheses in crucially different ways. The simplicity and explanatory power of an L-hypothesis often lead to its widespread acceptance even if it is not immediately capable of being put to an empirical test. With E-hypotheses, however, simplicity and explanatory power are not enough. Until the entities postulated by E-hypotheses are confirmed by hard experimental evidence, scientists tend, as in the case of quarks, to regard them as useful fictions.

The theistic hypothesis is definitely an E-hypothesis, not an L-hypothesis like the Newtonian model. Further, Swinburne is clearly claiming that God is more than a useful fiction. It is therefore quite inadequate to claim that simplicity and *post factum* explanatory efficacy are sufficient to confirm such a hypothesis.

A final way that Swinburne's theistic hypothesis diverges from the Newtonian model is with respect to its explanatory power. The great simplicity of Newton's laws only partially accounts for their rapid acceptance by his seventeenth-century contemporaries. Much (indeed most) of the reason for the initial acceptance of Newton's theory was that known laws, such as Kepler's laws of planetary motion and Galileo's law of falling bodies, could be *deduced* from that theory. Swinburne, on the other hand, freely admits that no facts about the world can be deduced from the theistic hypothesis. In fact, the most that he ever argues is that the probability that this universe will exist given that God exists—$p(e/h \cdot k)$, is not too low.[48] Hence, even the *post factum* explanatory power of the theistic hypothesis is quite low in comparison to the Newtonian model. This means that practically the entire support for Swinburne's hypothesis derives from its claimed simplicity. It would be highly instructive for Swinburne to adduce any example of an unquestionably scientific hypothesis that to a similar degree stakes its confirmation entirely upon the criterion of simplicity. Newton's laws of motion do not constitute such an example.

We have seen that Swinburne's claim that his theistic hypothesis parallels accepted scientific ones is open to serious question on a number of points. Swinburne claims that his arguments for theism are much like those that scientists employ when they argue for the existence of unobservable entities such as quarks. This is not so, however. Scientists have experimental evidence for quarks and, at the very least, did not feel compelled to accept them as real entities until such evidence was forthcoming.

Swinburne attempts to circumvent this objection by comparing his hypothesis with Newton's laws of motion. Newton's laws, though incapable of immediate empirical testing, were accepted because of their simplicity and ability to account for known phenomena. However, we have seen that Swinburne's hypothesis diverges widely from the Newtonian model. These divergences appear significant enough for a reasonable person to be justified in demanding more of the theistic hypothesis than the kind of support that Swinburne has so far offered.

Some doubts have been raised about Swinburne's project taken as a whole. Indeed, there are some alarming parallels between Swinburne's theistic hypothesis and the hypothesis of the "scientific creationists." Like the creationists, Swinburne offers an untestable hypothesis that is capable of making only unscientific *post factum* explanations. Hence, if Swinburne is claiming that his hypothesis is on all fours with unquestionably scientific ones, then he, like the creationists, is simply engaging in pseudoscience.

Perhaps, then, Swinburne would be ready to admit that his hypothesis does diverge rather far from any unquestionably scientific model. He might then contend that to deny strictly scientific status for his hypothesis does not deprive it of cogency. However, Swinburne must admit that his hypothesis will not enjoy confirmation of the same kind or degree as a well-confirmed scientific hypothesis. This means that he ought not to be surprised if his hypothesis fails to command consensus among the qualified discussants in the same way that a well-confirmed scientific hypothesis does. That is, he should admit from the start that there will be more room for rational dissent from his hypothesis than there currently is with respect to, say, quantum mechanics. To see exactly how cogent Swinburne's arguments are, each must be examined on its own merits. Hence, we now return to a detailed examination of his cosmological argument.

ASSESSING SWINBURNE'S ARGUMENT

We have seen that Swinburne repudiates the Principle of Sufficient Reason and the allied notion that some being can account for its own existence. Both Swinburne and the atheist hold that something exists as the brutally factual terminus of all explanation. Swinburne's cosmological argument entails the claim that God is a more satisfactory candidate for such a terminus than any other imaginable entity. In order to evaluate this claim we must first see exactly what it is that atheism leaves unexplained.

It is Swinburne's opinion that science has not yet put forward any solid reasons for thinking that either the universe had or did not have a beginning.[49] He therefore chooses to disregard the problem that arises for atheists only if the universe is of finite age, viz., the inexplicability of the initial state. Instead, he concentrates on the weakness that, he argues, afflicts all forms of atheism.

Swinburne contends that if scientific explanation is the only sort allowed, there can be no explanation for the entire series of the universe's states. Scientific explanation will only countenance explanations of the states of the universe in terms of the earlier states of the universe and the laws of nature. As we saw, Swinburne argues that the explanation of a sequence of states taken as a whole must be something that lies outside that sequence. Thus, if the sequence to be explained is the lighting of the fuse, the explosion of the dynamite, the collapse of the house, and Jones's death, the cause of that sequence as a whole is Smith's setting a match to the fuse. It is this requirement, that the explanation of an entire series be something outside the series, that Swinburne deploys against the Humean claim that if each member of a series is explained the series as a whole will be explained. Hence, if a whole series can be explained only by something outside the series, then clearly the set of states of the universe cannot be explained in terms of any member or members of that set. Swinburne concludes that atheism therefore leaves unexplained the existence of the universe over time, whether that time is of finite or infinite duration.

Now we do normally explain an entire causal series in terms of something outside that series. It is quite natural to speak of the cause of the sequence of events ending in Jones's death (the fuse being lit, the dynamite going off, the house collapsing) as simply being the fact that Smith set a match to the fuse. However, we must not forget that in grouping the above events together in the way that we have, we are performing what Hume called an "arbitrary act of the mind." To say that the above sequence as a whole lacks an explanation (suppose we did not know who lit the fuse) does not in the least vitiate the explanation of Jones's death in terms of the house collapsing. In fact, every event in our above sequence is perfectly well explained except the last, i.e., we know everything up to who lit the fuse. Further, what we *do* know in such a case is not one whit augmented when we come to know who lit the fuse: Smith was just as surely killed by the collapse of the house whether or not we ever know who lit the fuse.

The upshot of the above is that the inexplicability of a finite causal chain boils down to the inexplicability of its first term. Once that is given, the whole series is explained. It is therefore very hard to see how the atheist who holds that the universe is finite in age leaves anything unexplained except the initial state of the universe. To say that the series of states as a whole is unexplained just seems to say that *all* such states *are* explained but the first.

Suppose, though, that the universe is infinite in age, i.e., it lacks an initial state. Swinburne wants to argue that, since the causal chain stretches back infinitely, we cannot regard any past states of the universe as standing outside that chain. Thus, he argues that the infinite series of the universe's past states lacks explanation on the atheist's scheme.

But why not stand this argument on its head? That is, why not argue that *because* the past states of the universe constitute an infinite series (and thus, by definition, there cannot be any states standing outside of the series) the demand that it be explained in terms of something outside the series no longer applies? This argument seems plausible since in an infinite series, unlike a finite one, *each* state will *always* have an adequate explanation in terms of a preceding state. In fact, it is the very finitude of a finite series that makes us look beyond that series for its explanation. That is, because a finite series comes to an end, it will always stop short of the cause of the first member of that series. Hence, the first member will be unexplained and, as a result, the series as a whole will be unexplained. However, with an infinite series there will, by definition, be no first term and, it seems to follow, no reason to look beyond that series for an explanation of the series.

Further, as J. C. A. Gaskin notes, it is not at all clear what it means to speak of an infinite series "taken as a whole":

> It does not appear to me to make sense to talk about any sort of explanation (internal or external to the universe) of an *infinite* series of states considered "as a whole." No "whole series" of states exists to be explained. If a real infinite series means anything, it means a series incapable of being gathered as a whole—whatever whole you take, there is limitlessly more. It is *impossible* to take such a whole, and yet, every state has a sufficient explanation. [emphasis in original][50]

It seems, therefore, that the demand for an explanation of an infinitely old universe "as a whole" is either incoherent, or, if its coherence can be made out, does not demand an explanation in terms of anything "beyond" the universe.

What, then, does the atheist leave unexplained upon the sup-position that the universe is infinite in age? The permanent features of the universe mentioned by Swinburne, such as the amount of energy it contains, no longer seem to present any mystery. The universe presently contains the amount of energy it does because it contained just that amount of energy in each of its past states and the laws of conservation have always assured that just that amount was preserved as the states of the universe evolved. Of course, it is possible to *imagine* the universe all along having had a different amount of energy, but this does not create a mystery. *When* was it ever possible for the universe to have had a different amount of energy? On the supposition that the universe is infinitely old such a possibility has simply never arisen.

Also, what are we to make of Swinburne's accusation that atheists who propose an infinitely old universe leave unexplained "the non-existence of a time before which there was no universe"?[51] It is hard to know what to make of this statement because it seems scarcely intelligible. At any rate, the nonexistence of anything does not present a mystery unless we have some reason to think that it *should* exist. The nonexistence of a rhinoceros in my bedroom is not a mystery that requires explanation; there simply is no reason to think that a rhinoceros ought to be in my bedroom. Likewise, unless we have some reason to think there should have been a time before the universe existed, the nonexistence of such a time just is not a problem.

Perhaps, though, the real battle line between theists and atheists ought to be whether and how the laws of nature can be explained. Even if an infinite succession of states does not in itself present any problems, what atheists still leave unexplained are the laws of nature that govern the transition from one state to another.[52] For instance, it does not seem that atheists can explain why the universe has the particular set of laws it has or why those laws remain constant over time.

Before proceeding we need to be clear about the effect, if any, on Swinburne's position if atheists concede that they cannot explain the ultimate laws of nature, whatever they might be. Swinburne endorses what he calls a "powers and liabilities" account of the laws of nature.[53] He argues, plausibly, that we must not make the mistake of thinking of the laws of nature as extra entities that somehow exist alongside material bodies. That is, the laws of nature are not *things* but rather powers and liabilities possessed by material objects:

> A power of a body is a capacity of it to bring about effects. A liability of a body is a disposition of it to suffer change under various cir-cumstances—among the liabilities of a body are that it has (of physical necessity or probability) to exercise its power when subjected to various stimuli. Thus instead of saying that the ignition of a certain mass of gunpowder plus a natural law of chemistry explained some explosion, earlier scientists would have said that the gunpowder caused the explo-sion, the power to cause an explosion being among the powers of the gunpowder, and a liability necessarily to exercise that power when ignited being among the liabilities of gunpowder; and the explosion was to be explained by the gunpowder's exercising its powers in virtue of its liabilities.[54]

Hence, for Swinburne, to say that a law of nature is unexplained is to say that there is no explanation of why a certain material body possesses the particular powers and liabilities that it has. Of course, the powers and liabilities of one body may be explained in terms of the powers and liabilities of constituent bodies and those in turn by even more fundamental entities. Presumably, though, rock bottom is eventually reached. At present, rock bottom would be the powers

and liabilities of such entities as quarks and electrons. Since, by
definition, the ultimate features of the universe will constitute the
ultimate terms of scientific explanation, science clearly cannot account
for those absolutely basic features. Hence, atheists must concede that
they cannot explain why the ultimate laws of nature are as they are.
In Swinburne's terms they cannot explain why the fundamental
constituents of the universe, whatever they might be, have the characteristic powers and liabilities that they do.

What, though, does this concession really amount to? To say
that there is no explanation of why a quark, given that it is a fundamental particle, has the powers and liabilities it possesses, seems
tantamount to saying that there is no explanation of why a quark
is a quark. Surely anything with a different set of powers and liabilities
than those possessed by quarks would simply not be a quark. After
all, what is a fundamental particle over and above a particular set
of irreducible powers and liabilities? It appears, therefore, that when
our inquiries have reached the fundamental stuff of nature, and hence
the terminus of scientific explanation, there just is not anything left
to be explained. Quarks are just quarks; that is the bottom line.

Perhaps this misses the point. Maybe the difficulty is not that
quarks, given that they do in fact exist and that they are fundamental
particles, have the powers and liabilities they have. Rather, the question
is why quarks exist in the first place rather than something else or
perhaps nothing at all. However, it must be recalled that on the
hypothesis of an infinitely old universe there is no "in the first place"
when it was possible for nothing or something else to exist instead
of what does in fact exist. Of course, it is conceivable that nothing
or something different might have existed. But again, it is difficult
to see how this creates problems for the atheist. If the universe has
always existed, then it has never been possible for there to be nothing
or for something else to exist.

In conclusion, on the hypothesis that the universe is infinitely
old, atheism appears to explain everything that can reasonably be
thought explicable. Each state of the universe is explained by a previous
state and the laws of nature. The demand to know the cause of
the set of states "as a whole" is incoherent, or, if allowed, does not
require an answer in terms of anything transcending the universe.
The laws of nature reduce in the final analysis to the powers and
liabilities of the fundamental physical stuff. The demand to know

why the ultimate physical stuff has the powers and liabilities it has is incoherent. This is because the fundamental stuff just would not be *that* stuff if its powers and liabilities were different. Finally, though we can imagine there never having been anything or there all along having been something else in existence, the presuppositon that our universe has always existed explains why these other "possibilities" were never actualized.

If the atheistic hypothesis thus explains everything that can be explained, why should a theistic hypothesis ever be invoked? The only possible answer seems to be that *as a total system* theism will be simpler than atheism. In other words, as ultimate theories of existence theism and atheism both adequately explain the totality of things, but theism does so with greater simplicity than does atheism.

This, however, seems plainly false. If we presume that the universe is infinitely old, the universe, in all of its complexity, will have always existed on both the theistic and the atheistic accounts. However, on the theistic hypothesis something else, namely, God, will have also always existed. Further, the theist must also postulate a power continuously exercised by God to keep the universe in existence (otherwise God just exits in parallel with the universe and has no creative input with respect to it). Unless it can be shown that the universe somehow *needs* to be kept in existence, Swinburne's theism thus seems to be a paradigm case of multiplying entities beyond necessity.

It appears that if Swinburne's cosmological argument is to have any chance of making headway, it must presuppose that the universe is finite in age. That is, it must first assume that the cosmos had an initial state and then argue that God is a more acceptable terminus of explanation than that initial state.

Whereas classical systems of atheism, such as the Roman poet Lucretius's great *De rerum natura,* presupposed the eternal existence of matter, most atheists would now likely be willing to accept that the universe had a first state. This is because the bulk of scientific opinion, despite Swinburne's earlier-mentioned skeptical reservations, now appears to favor some sort of "big bang" cosmology. That is, various converging lines of evidence seem to indicate that the entire cosmos, indeed space-time itself, originated instantaneously in a primeval explosion occurring some fifteen to twenty billion years ago.[55] Further, "big bang" cosmologists believe that the current state of the universe—its configuration, its laws, and the entities that constitute it—are all explicable in terms of events that occurred within the first split seconds of the universe's existence. Indeed, some physicists hold out the hope that particle physics and "big bang" cosmology will soon be united under a single theory that will show how the four basic forces of nature evolved from a single "superforce" believed to have existed in the first explosive instant. The boldest theorists are pushing even further by offering scenarios that would explain how the universe arose uncaused, literally *ex nihilo*.

Of course, even the most optimistic of the cutting-edge cosmologists admit that their wilder ideas are still entirely speculative. More cautious physicists point out that the models so far offered stretch accepted theories and concepts far beyond their tested range of application. Some philosophers are more skeptical still.[56]

Fortunately, our interests here do not turn on the question of whether science will ever achieve the sort of ultimate success that presently eludes the searchers for "superforce." Swinburne clearly holds that no matter how successful science is at explaining phenomena, it will always be warranted to pass beyond science to theistic explanation. In other words, Swinburne holds that theism provides a more acceptable stopping-place for explanation than any *possible* scientific theory. This being so, it will here be assumed that the boldest aspirations of science will in fact be rewarded with success. That is, it will be taken for granted that science can succeed in showing that all natural phenomena are ultimately explicable in terms of a single theory lying at the apex of all hierarchies of scientific explanation. In such a case, all that the atheist will have to regard as permanently inexplicable will be the ultimate terms of that ultimate theory. Swinburne's job is therefore to show that God is a more acceptable terminus of explanation than any such conjectured ultimate scientific explanation.

To get right to the point, why is it better to end explanation with God than, say, with an uncaused first state of the universe? Perhaps God is simpler than any conceivable initial physical state and therefore a priori more likely to exist uncaused. We have seen that much of the reason for God's claimed simplicity is that his attributes are infinite in quality. Swinburne apparently assumes that no physical entity could possess such infinite properties and therefore cannot emulate God with respect to simplicity. Physicist Paul Davies directly addresses such an assumption:

According to our best scientific understanding of the primeval universe it does indeed seem as though the universe began in the simplest state of all—thermodynamic equilibrium—and that the currently observed complex structures and elaborate activity only appeared subsequently. It might then be argued that the primeval universe is, in fact, the simplest thing that we can imagine. Moreover, if the prediction of an initial singularity is taken at face value, the universe began in a state of infinite temperature, infinite density, and infinite energy. Is this not at least as plausible as infinite mind?[57]

In short, it does in fact seem that naturalistic hypotheses can emulate (or surpass) theism with respect to simplicity. Even the possession of infinite attributes is not a privilege restricted to God alone.

At any rate, what is it about unlimited attributes that prevents them from crying out for explanation in the same way that limited ones supposedly do? In other words, why should the possession of unlimited attributes *ipso facto* make a being simpler than one having limited properties? Swinburne is not much help here. As we have seen, all he tells us is that

an omnipotent God is a simpler hypothesis than the hypothesis that there is a God who has such-and-such limited power . . . it is simpler in just the same way that the hypothesis that some particle has zero mass or infinite velocity is simpler than the hypothesis that it has a mass of 0.34127 of some unit, or a velocity 301,000 km/sec. A finite limitation cries out for explanation of why there is just that particular limit, in a way that limitlessness does not.[58]

Unquestionably, a hypothesis postulating zero power for some entity will, other things being equal, be simpler than one postulating some degree of power. Zero power just means no power at all, and, as noted earlier, the nonexistence of something does not demand any explanation unless there is some reason that it should exist. However, with respect to infinite power, Swinburne's claim seems to be that it lacks a particularity or definiteness possessed by finite degrees of power. But, on the contrary, omnipotence seems to be a highly specific and determinate degree of power, viz., the highest logically possible degree of power. If omnipotence is thus a particular, determinate level of power, it is not clear why it would fail to demand explanation just as much as any other degree of power. The alternative would be to deny that omnipotence is a specific degree of power.

It seems, though, that power just is the sort of attribute that must be possessed in some degree or other if it is to be possessed at all. To say that something has power but does not have it in some specific degree does not make sense.

For the sake of argument, let us suppose that it can be shown that the theistic hypothesis is simpler than any possible naturalistic hypothesis. This leads us to the most central question for Swinburne's entire project: Why is it more likely that the ultimate, uncaused entity will be a simple rather complex entity? Anthony O'Hear has said all that needs to be said here:

> Against what standard of probability can we possibly judge in general terms what type of thing is most likely to exist? If experience is anything to go by, and what is *likely* to exist in the abstract is rather like what we do have experience of as existing, then we will have to conclude that what is likely to exist is rather more complex than it need be. (We can easily imagine possible worlds a lot simpler than ours. . . .) If, on the other hand, we do not take our actual experience into account, we might wonder what the probability assessment is being based on. It hardly seems reasonable to say, in the absence of any evidence, that what is most likely to exist is that possible world which the human mind finds more simple. Indeed, in the absence of any way of deciding what is correct here, one doubts whether the question has any meaning at all. In a way, the point being made is the old one made by Peirce, that universes are not as plentiful as blackberries, that, in other words, we have no sample of universes to inspect to infer what is a priori more likely or unlikely in an actual world.[59]

O'Hear's remarks have the ring of finality. However, his insights are so important and so succinctly expressed that it would be worthwhile to expand on them. How can we possibly know what is likely or unlikely to exist as the ultimate, inexplicable brute fact? What grounds could anyone have for saying, as Swinburne does, that the simpler something is, the likelier it is to exist uncaused?

Perhaps our previous experience should guide us. That is, if scientists have succeeded in finding ever simpler and more comprehensive theories, then perhaps we can project that the ultimate, most comprehensive theory will be the simplest of all. Indeed, much of the history of science is the story of how baffling complexity has been made explicable in terms of underlying simplicity. We have already seen how Newton's laws of motion provided simple explanations for the behavior of comets, carriages, cannonballs, and very many other diverse objects. Similarly, an enormous number of puzzling biological phenomena can be made comprehensible in the simple terms of Darwin's theory of natural selection. Perhaps, then, we can extrapolate from the history of science and predict that the deepest reality, the final term of all explanations, will be the simplest sort of thing that can be.

There are a number of problems with basing the claim of ultimate simplicity upon the history of science. First, that history has not been one of uniform progress toward greater and greater simplicity. Indeed, the usual course of events is for simple theories to experience enormous success at first and then to run into difficulties that require their qualification or modification. When quarks were first proposed it was thought that only three quarks would explain all the observed properties of hadrons. Since that time further experimental data have called for the postulation of a fourth, fifth, and perhaps a sixth quark. Thus, initially simple hypotheses tend to become more complex as science progresses. Of course, if a theory becomes *too* cumbersome, scientists will search for a simpler theory to replace it. However, when such new theories are found, they usually undergo a process of complexification as well.

Another problem with using the history of science to support the theistic hypothesis is that Swinburne has specifically excluded all nontautological knowledge from the background knowledge upon which his hypothesis is to be judged.[60] The fact that scientists have often discovered underlying simplicity is presumably a part of that excluded background and so cannot apply to the evaluation of Swinburne's hypothesis.

If, on the other hand, such nontautological background is allowed, much of that information might count heavily against the theistic hypothesis. For instance, science has never yet come across a single instance of a disembodied mind. Hence, part of our scientific background knowledge is that the probability of there being a disembodied mind is very low. If the background knowledge upon which the theistic hypothesis is to be judged includes the knowledge that science often discovers simplicity, why should it not also include the knowledge that disembodied minds are very unlikely? Since God is supposed to be just such a disembodied mind, it seems that the inclusion of such background knowledge would count heavily against the theistic hypothesis.

Finally, and most importantly, even if the history of science had been a uniform march of progress in the acquisition of ever-simpler theories, it does not follow that simplicity per se can be used as a guide to ultimate reality. Just because the truth is simple does not mean that what is simple is true. Indeed, one very important lesson to learn from the history of science is that the laborious process of testing, observing, and experimenting cannot be circumvented by appeals to beauty, simplicity, or any other such nonempirical criterion.[61] It never hurts to be reminded of what T. H. Huxley called the greatest of tragedies: a grand and beautiful theory destroyed by an ugly little fact. Since ugly little facts have a way of cropping up at the most inopportune moments, we should perhaps be suspicious of theories that are too simple or too beautiful. They may be too good to be true.

If the history of science cannot support the claim that the simplicity of a theoretical entity enhances the probability that it will exist uncaused, we must again ask just how that claim can be supported. The fact is that we are not in a position to observe universes coming into being. If we were, if we could witness the spontaneous, uncaused births of many universes, we might be in a position to judge what sorts of realities are likely to exist uncaused. However, since we are not in such a position, we seem to have no empirical basis for judging what is likely to exist uncaused.

If no empirical grounds can be given, perhaps Swinburne bases his claims solely on logical grounds. However, it is very difficult to see what those could be. Can it be shown that there are more simple possible universes than complex ones? Prima facie there would seem to be an infinite number of both types. Even if we could know that the class of simple possible universes has more members than the class of complex possible universes, can we know that individuals of one type are just as likely to become actual as individuals of another type? If, for instance, each possible complex universe has a much greater chance of becoming the actual universe than each possible simple universe, it might not matter if the possible simple universes outnumber the complex ones.

If all of this talk about the likelihood of a possible universe becoming actual seems absurd, that is precisely the point. Again, we simply do not seem to be in a position to judge a priori what kind of possible universe is more likely to be the actual one. Timothy

Ferris has made a similar point about the difficulty of making estimates of the likelihood that intelligent life might exist on other planets:

> One cannot reliably calculate the odds of a particular thing having happened unless one either understands the process—that is, can properly identify and quantify all the variables involved—or has an adequate experimental data base from which to draw phenomenological information about it. If, for instance, we want to predict how close an intercontinental ballistic missile will land to its intended target, we can calculate all the variables—the flight characteristics of the missile, the influences of environment on its navigational system, etc.—or we can test real missiles, as often as possible, in order to generate a data base about how they perform. In practice one does both, since both approaches may err. But when the question involves intelligent life arising on other planets, we can with confidence do neither, since we have only a rudimentary understanding of the variables involved, and none whatsoever regarding the statistics.[62]

With respect to possible worlds becoming actual we know even less than we do about the likelihood of intelligent life existing on other planets. We know nothing about the process involved and nothing about the relative frequencies with which different possible universes become actual.

It therefore appears that no objective reasons can be given in support of the claim that the simpler an entity is, the more likely it is to exist uncaused. What, then, are we to make of the fact that some confirmation theorists *do* recommend that a higher a priori probability be accorded to hypotheses that, other things being equal, are simpler than competing hypotheses? Other confirmation theorists, including, most notably, Karl Popper, do not make this recommendation. (Even those who do would likely be very surprised to learn that they thereby implicitly endorse grandiose metaphysical theses about the nature of Ultimate Existence!) How then do we account for the scientific preference for simple hypotheses?

The answer is that simplicity is a desired feature of hypotheses, not because of the nature of reality, but because of the nature of science. As O'Hear puts it:

> Science aims at more than truth; it aims also at a system of simple and wide-ranging hypotheses. Without such a preference, scientists would have no reason for preferring theories that postulate underlying

unifying causes for diverse phenomena, rather than remaining content with mere summaries or digests of past observations. For similar reasons, preference may be accorded theories which postulate one entity, rather than many, one kind of entity rather than many kinds, and zero or infinite degrees of a given quality rather than some intermediate figure. Some may indeed be prepared to mark these preferences by according theories which are simpler in these respects greater degreees of prior probability. . . .[63]

In other words, it is an (if not *the*) aim of science to make systematic sense of the jumble of apparently disjointed and unconnected events we encounter in experience. Metaphorically speaking, science endeavors to reveal hidden conspiracies in nature—unsuspected relations and regularities that permit a unified explanation of diverse phenomena. In this sense, scientific explanation just *is* simplification. However, it must be emphasized that such simplification is one of the *aims* of science; there is no prior assurance that such hopes will meet with complete success. There just is no way of knowing a priori whether the ultimate terms of explanation will turn out to be as simple as they could be. The preference for simple hypotheses therefore appears to arise from the fundamental aims of science, not from a misplaced trust in how reality will ultimately turn out.

In conclusion, it seems that Swinburne has given no reason to think that the ultimate, uncaused existent is more likely to be God than the universe. Indeed, he has given us no reason to think that meaningful probabilities *can* be assigned to claims about ultimate, uncaused existence. That is, he has not shown that any meaningful intrinsic or a priori probabilities can be assigned to naturalism or theism. In Bayesian terms, Swinburne has given us no basis for assigning *any* probability (high or low) to $p(h/k)$ or $p(e/k)$. If no simple probabilities can be defined, Bayes's theorem cannot be employed to determine complex probabilities.

It follows that the "relevance condition" cannot be met; there is no way to ascertain whether $p(e/h \cdot k) > p(e/\sim h \cdot k)$. The latter probability, $p(e/\sim h \cdot k)$, is the probability that the universe will exist given that God does not exist. This probability is equal to the probability that the universe exists uncaused, $p(e/k)$, plus the probability that the universe was created by some being other than God. But if $p(e/k)$ is undefined, $p(e/\sim h \cdot k)$ must be also. In other words, there is no way to show that the universe is more likely to exist given that God exists than it is given that God does not exist. This means that it cannot be shown that the universe is evidence for the existence of God, and so Swinburne's version of the cosmological argument does not work.

NOTES

1. For excellent criticisms of the creationists see Douglas J. Futuyma, *Science on Trial* (New York: Pantheon Books, 1981), and Philip Kitcher, *Abusing Science* (Cambridge, Mass.: MIT Press, 1982).

2. The best edition of Hume's *Dialogues* is the one edited by Norman Kemp Smith (New York: Macmillan, 1986).

3. Richard Swinburne, *The Existence of God* (Oxford, England: Clarendon Press, 1979); hereafter abbreviated as *EOG*.

4. One classic statement of the traditional cosmological argument is found in G. W. Leibniz, *On the Ultimate Origination of Things,* trans. M. Morris, in *The Philosophical Writings of Leibniz* (London: Everyman, 1934), pp. 31f.

5. J. L. Mackie, *The Miracle of Theism* (Oxford, England: Clarendon Press, 1982), p, 85.

6. See Terence Penelhum, *Religion and Rationality* (New York: Random House, 1971), pp. 35–47.

7. See *The Miracle of Theism,* pp. 41–63.

8. Swinburne, *EOG,* p. 128.

9. See Swinburne's *An Introduction to Confirmation Theory* (London: Methuen, 1973).

10. The clearest introduction to Bayes's theorem and the probability calculus in general is in Brian Skyrms, *Choice and Chance,* 3d ed. (Belmont, Calif.: Wadsworth, 1986), pp. 129–58.

11. Swinburne, *EOG,* p. 90.

12. See Alvin Plantinga, "The Probabilistic Argument from Evil," *Philosophical Studies* 35 (1979): 19–30.

13. Swinburne distinguishes between what he calls "C-inductive" and "P-inductive" arguments (*EOG,* p. 7). The former only serve to raise the probability of a proposition; the latter make that proposition more probable than not. Swinburne only claims that his cosmological argument is C-inductive (*EOG,* p. 131).

14. Swinburne, *EOG,* p. 131.

15. Ibid., p. 116.

16. David Hume, *Dialogues Concerning Natural Religion,* in *Hume On Religion,* ed. Richard Wollheim (London: Fontana, 1963), p. 164.

17. This example comes from Paul Edwards.

18. Swinburne, *EOG,* p. 122. "Complete" and "full" explanations are technical terms for Swinburne (see pp. 22–24 and pp. 73–75). Unfortunately, his definitions of these terms are extremely convoluted and unilluminating. As far as I can tell, a "full" explanation of an event E is one that mentions all of the factors (entities, initial conditions, laws of nature, etc.) that are jointly sufficient to bring E about. An event E is "completely" explained if it is fully explained at a given time, but none of the factors in terms of which E is explained can themselves be explained in terms of further factors operating at that time.

19. Ibid., pp. 123–24.

20. Ibid., p. 124.

21. Ibid.

22. Ibid., pp 124–25.

23. Ibid., p, 128.

24. Ibid., pp. 287–88.

25. Ibid.p. 130.

26. Swinburne's clearest definition is found in his reply to Mackie's criticism of his cosmological argument: "Mackie, Induction, and God," *Religious Studies* 19 (1983): 386.

27. Swinburne summarizes his views on the factors affecting a priori probability in *EOG,* pp. 51–57.

28. Ibid., p. 65.

29. Ibid., p. 129.

30. Swinburne explains his reasons for the simplicity of theism in detail in *EOG,* pp. 90–102.

31. Ibid., p. 94.

32. Ibid., pp. 94–95.

33. Ibid., p. 95.

34. Ibid., pp. 96–97.

35. Ibid., pp. 97–102.

36. Ibid., p. 131.

37. Swinburne, "Mackie, Induction, and God," p. 386.

38. This problem and how quark theory has resolved it are brilliantly explained by Chris Quigg, "Elementary Particles and Forces," *Scientific American* 252, no. 4 (April 1985): 84–95.

39. Richard Morris, *Dismantling the Universe* (New York: Simon and Schuster, 1983), p. 195.

40. Ibid.

41. Quigg, "Elementary Particles and Forces," pp. 86–87.

42. Ibid., p. 84.

43. Swinburne, *EOG,* pp. 66–67.

44. Ibid., p. 67.

45. See Ronald Giere, *Understanding Scientific Reasoning* (New York: Holt, Rinehart, and Winston, 1984), pp. 158–63.

46. Bertrand Russell, *Religion and Science* (New York: Henry Holt, 1935).

47. Carl G. Hempel, *Philosophy of Natural Science* (Englewood Cliffs, N.J.: Prentice-Hall, 1966), p. 30.

48. Swinburne, *EOG,* p. 131.

49. Ibid., p. 121.

50. J. C. A. Gaskin, *The Quest for Eternity* (New York: Penguin Books, 1984), p. 63.

51. Swinburne, *EOG,* p. 124.

52. Ibid., p. 126.

53. Ibid., pp. 42–44.

54. Ibid., p. 43.

55. For an introduction to "big bang" cosmology see one of the following: Timothy Ferris, *Coming of Age in the Milky Way* (New York: William Morrow, 1988); Heinz Pagels, *Perfect Symmetry* (New York: Simon and Schuster, 1985); Marcia Bartusiak, *Thursday's Universe* (New York: Times Books, 1986).

56. See Patrick Suppes, *Probabilistic Metaphysics* (Don Mills, Ontario: Oxford University Press, 1984).

57. Paul Davies, *God and the New Physics* (New York: Penguin Books, 1986), p. 49.

58. Swinburne, *EOG,* p. 94.

59. Anthony O'Hear, *Experience, Explanation, and Faith* (London: Routledge and Kegan Paul, 1984), pp. 116–17.

60. Swinburne, *EOG,* p. 90.

61. A good critique of the appeal to simplicity and other such a priori criteria is found in Rom Harré, *The Anticipation of Nature* (London: Hutchinson, 1965).

62. Ferris, *Coming of Age in the Milky Way,* p. 373.

3

Evil and the Burden of Proof

In the first chapter we saw that the burden of proof cannot be evaded by anyone who wants to argue the truth of theism. In chapter 2 we looked at one prominent recent effort to bear that burden of proof. We concluded that that effort has failed. Of course, many other arguments have been offered for the existence of God, but even theistic philosophers cannot agree on whether any of them is sound. Indeed, the failure of Swinburne's strongest arguments bodes ill for all such efforts.

Paradoxically, the efforts of Plantinga and Swinburne may have left the atheist in a stronger position than ever. The existence of God is not a basic belief for the atheist, and Plantinga has said nothing to make him believe that he is irrational in not having such a basic belief. Indeed, Plantinga's Calvinist epistemology seems to assure the atheist that, if he is careful in selecting his paradigms of proper basicality, he need have little fear of being argued into belief. Further, the latest and most sophisticated efforts to provide arguments for God's existence are now seen to fare no better than earlier attempts. The atheist therefore seems fully justified in denying that there are any grounds for belief in the existence of God.

Suppose, though, that the atheist is not satisfied with a purely defensive posture. Suppose atheists want to see if they can bear a burden of proof in arguing against theism. In other words, can atheists go on the offensive and provide reasons, arguments, or evidence *against* belief in the existence of God (reasons, arguments, or evidence, that is, that do more than simply point out, à la Hanson, that there are no good reasons *for* believing in God)?

Through the centuries, the most popular such "atheological" argument has been the so-called problem of evil, which has often been posed as the charge that theists contradict themselves. Theists conceive of God as omnipotent and perfectly good. "Omnipotent" means "all-powerful." To say that God is omnipotent is usually taken to mean that God can do anything he wants (so long as he doesn't want something that is logically impossible, like making one plus one equal three). To say that God is perfectly good is usually taken to mean that God opposes evil and wants to end it. Further, it is undoubtedly the case that evil exists.

It therefore appears that the theist is committed to each of the following claims:

(1) God is omnipotent.

(2) God is perfectly good.

(3) Evil exists.

But, so the argument goes, these three claims form an inconsistent set, i.e., if you believe any two of them, you have to reject the third. Thus, if God has the power to eliminate evil, but evil still exists, it must follow that he does not *want* to eliminate evil. But in that case he cannot be perfectly good. On the other hand, if God wants to eliminate evil, but evil still exists, it must be the case that God *cannot* eliminate evil. But then he cannot be omnipotent. Finally, if God wants to eliminate evil and has the power to do so, evil will not exist. But evil does exist, and so we have to reject either the claim that God is omnipotent or the claim that God is perfectly good. However, since omnipotence and perfect goodness are part of the *definition* of the term 'God', to surrender either of these claims is to surrender belief in God. Hence, the existence of evil seems to disprove the existence of God.

As it stands, the above argument is not decisive against theism. As Nelson Pike has pointed out, it is clearly possible for a perfectly good being to allow certain evils to exist.[1] For example, a perfectly good parent could allow a child to suffer the pain of an inoculation since the slight pain of the procedure is protection against the much greater pain of disease. Of course, to suffer unwanted and undeserved pain is always bad. However, Pike's example shows that there are circumstances in which someone who has inflicted pain would not be held morally blameworthy. Thus, a perfectly good being might be morally justified in permitting the existence of certain evils.

It follows that the existence of evil does not disprove the existence of God unless it can be shown that God is not morally justified in allowing evil to exist. But, Pike asks, how can we ever be certain that this last claim is true?[2] Of course, at present we might not *see* how certain evils could be justified, but this is no reason to think that they *cannot* be justified. That is, no matter how apparently pointless or unnecessary an evil might presently seem to us, we allegedly have no way of proving that it cannot ultimately be justified.

It therefore seems that the atheist is doomed to frustration in his effort to derive a contradiction from the theist's beliefs about God and evil. No matter what evils the atheist mentions, the theist can maintain that it has not been proven that those evils will remain unjustified throughout eternity. Of course, the theist might not be able to specify what *would* serve to justify certain evils, but this does not mean that he is irrational in holding that they *can* ultimately be justified.

Pike's reply does not settle the issue, however. Some atheist philosophers have risen to Pike's challenge and have argued that it can be shown that God has no morally adequate justification for permitting evil. Two such philosophers are J. L. Mackie and Antony Flew.[3] We turn now to their arguments.

THE ATHEOLOGICAL ATTACK:
THE CHARGE OF INCONSISTENCY

Mackie and Flew begin by asking what sort of morally adequate justification *could* excuse God's permission of evil. They note that the traditional answer to this question—at least as it pertains to human evil—is that God has endowed human beings with free will and that moral evil is the result of misuse of this great gift. This argument, the "Free-Will Defense" (FWD for short), runs as follows: God could have created a universe populated entirely by innocent automata—robotlike beings that have been programmed always to do what is right. However, such a universe would be devoid of *moral* good. Moral goodness results from a *free* choice to do what is right; an act cannot be morally good if it is performed by someone who could not have done otherwise. Hence, a universe that contains moral goodness *must* contain agents endowed with the power to choose between morally significant alternatives. It follows that God could not have created a universe containing moral goodness but no free agents any more than he could have created a universe containing squares but no four-sided figures.

However, the FWD continues, to possess free will means that one must also possess the power to misuse that free will. Hence, a universe that contains moral goodness will be a universe containing creatures that have the power to misuse their freedom and so commit acts of moral evil. It follows that God cannot be blamed if the creatures in such a universe do misuse their freedom, as they sometimes will, by doing what is evil. Further, moral good is good of such a high order that a universe containing moral good and some moral evil will be better than a universe containing no moral good and no moral evil. The FWD concludes that God is therefore justified in creating a universe that contains moral evil since the omission of such evil would have necessitated the omission of moral goodness also.

A number of objections have been made against the FWD. First and most obviously, it seems to leave unaccounted for a vast amount of evil. Much pain and suffering appear to have their source in impersonal natural causes rather than in the choices of free agents. Earthquakes, disease, floods, birth defects, and the like are explicable in terms of the impersonal operation of the laws of nature. Therefore, the FWD, at best, only accounts for *moral* evil; it seems to have no bearing on the explanation of *natural* evil.

Further, it is often pointed out that freedom of the will does not have the sort of absolute value attributed to it by proponents of the FWD. Suppose that a man, of his own free will, decides to make his living by robbing banks. In this case we think it quite right and proper for the authorities to interfere with the exercise of this person's free choices. Indeed, we would blame them if they failed to do so. Hence, there are times when the failure to *limit* someone's free choices is a great moral evil.

Mackie and Flew raise a much more radical objection against the FWD. They argue that God could have created a universe populated by beings who always freely choose to do good. That is, they deny that all of the free agents that God could have created are such that they will inevitably choose to commit some evils. After all, it might be added, are not the angels supposed to be free yet sinless, as are the saved in heaven? If, therefore, God could have populated the universe with free beings who choose never to do wrong, there seems to be no morally adequate justification for his not having done so. Mackie expresses the argument this way:

> If God has made men such that in their free choices they sometimes prefer what is good and sometimes what is evil, why could he not have made men such that they always freely choose the good? If there is no logical impossibility in a man's freely choosing the good on one, or on several occasions, there cannot be a logical impossibility in his freely choosing the good on every occasion. God was not, then, faced with a choice between making innocent automata and making beings who, in acting freely, would sometimes go wrong: there was open to him the obviously better possibility of making beings who would act freely but always go right. Clearly his failure to avail himself of this possibility is inconsistent with his being both omnipotent and wholly good.[4]

Elsewhere, Mackie gives an even more succinct expression of this argument:

> Since there seems to be no reason why an omnipotent, omniscient, and wholly good god would not have preferred this alternative [the creation of agents who always freely choose to do good], the theist who maintains that there is such a god, and yet that he did not opt for this—since by his own account human beings make bad free choices—seems to be committed to an inconsistent set of assertions.[5]

Flew's argument is very similar, but he recognizes that he must begin by elucidating the concepts of "acting freely" and "being free to choose."[6] He argues that to say that a particular action was freely chosen does not mean that it was uncaused or unpredictable. For instance, the decision of two people to get married is properly described as a free choice even if that decision was predictable:

A paradigm case of acting freely, of being free to choose, would be the marriage of two normal young people, when there was no question of the parties "having to get married," and no social or parental pressure on either of them: a case which happily is scarcely rare. To say that Murdo was free to ask whichever eligible girl of his acquaintance he wanted, and that he chose to ask, and was accepted by, and has now married Mairi of his own free will, is not to say that his actions and choices were uncaused or in principle unpredictable: but precisely and only that, being of an age to know his own mind, he did what he did and rejected possible alternative courses of action without being under any pressure to act in this way. Indeed those who know Murdo and Mairi may have known what was going to happen long before the day of the wedding.[7]

It is important to note the way that Flew argues here. One of the most basic tenets of recent analytic philosophy holds that the meanings of linguistic expressions are not to be settled by philosophical fiat, but by an examination of the actual employment of such expressions in natural languages.[8] That is, we settle questions about the meaning of a given locution by developing "paradigm-case arguments"—arguments that appeal to concrete examples that exemplify the typical employment of that locution. Hence, we determine the meaning of such expressions as 'being free to choose' by looking at typical cases in which a native speaker of the language would describe an action as freely chosen.

Flew contends that one such paradigm case is the marriage of Mairi and Murdo; if any action is freely chosen, this one is. After all, it is not a "shotgun" wedding, and it is stipulated that neither party is under any undue parental or societal pressure to get married. However, notes Flew, to say that Mairi and Murdo freely chose to marry does not, in ordinary language, bear the connotation that their choice was uncaused or unpredictable.[9] Indeed, friends and relatives may have secretly predicted it long before Murdo and Mairi made the decision. Further, their decision to marry may have been completely determined by such causal factors as their being in love, their desire to have children, their desire for companionship, their desire for a steady sex partner, etc. However, the fact that their mutual decision was determined by such factors does not lead people to stop saying that their marriage was freely chosen. Indeed, it is precisely when people marry for such reasons that we *do* say that they freely chose to marry.

The upshot is that Flew regards ordinary language as embodying a notion of free choice that is entirely consistent with the predictability or causal determination of such choices. That is, Flew sees the *meaning* of such terms as 'free choice'—meanings established by paradigm-case arguments—as being wholly compatible with their being causally determined. The position espoused by Flew, and, he claims, the one embodied in ordinary language, is therefore called "compatibilism." For the compatibilist, to say that someone's choice was free is to say that it was caused by that person's own desires, character, beliefs, etc., and that that person was in no way coerced, manipulated, or otherwise excessively externally or internally pressured into that decision.

With respect to the FWD, Flew's compatibility thesis implies that

> if it really is logically possible for an action to be both freely chosen and yet fully determined by caused causes, then the keystone argument of the Free-will Defense, that there is a contradiction in speaking of God so arranging the laws of nature that all men always as a matter of fact freely choose to do the right, cannot hold.[10]

In other words, since our free choices are determined by our characters, desires, beliefs, etc., God could have arranged things so that such decision-determining factors always produced good decisions. That is, we could have been placed in an environment that would have molded our characters, desires, beliefs, etc., so that we would always freely choose the good. In short, it is not a logical necessity that free creatures will inevitably decide to commit evils. It is, at most, a contingent necessity, and all contingent matters are, Flew assumes, under God's control. It therefore appears that God cannot have a morally adequate justification for not having created a world populated with creatures who always freely choose the good.

At this point someone might object: "Surely this is a specious argument. If God were surreptitiously to arrange things so that our characters, desires, beliefs, etc., would be determined in ways that would produce only good choices, he would be the Great Hypnotist and we would be his unwitting dupes. That is, we would have the illusion that we were acting freely when in fact we would only be acting out a massive charade. Although we would think that *we* were making our own decisions, we would in fact have been preprogrammed and so could not have acted other than we did act. Hence, since the ability to have acted otherwise is a necessary condition for moral goodness, Flew's world would be one without moral goodness. Hence, God *is* justified in not having created such a world."

The above objection is based upon an ambiguity in the phrase "could have acted otherwise." I wore my brown suit today. I could have done otherwise; I could have worn my blue suit. On this last claim both Flew and the above objector would agree. However, the objector construes this as implying that at the moment of decision— as I stood towel draped in front of my clothes closet—my decision to wear the brown suit was determined by nothing but my own completely uncaused choices. That is, my choice of the brown suit is not determined by external factors, such as discovering a tear in the sleeve of the blue suit, or by involuntary internal factors, such as happening to fancy the brown suit that day. Clearly, on such a construal, my ability to do otherwise is incompatible with my choice having been in any sense caused or determined by anything outside of me. Hence, the objector takes an "incompatibilist" view of the relation between causal determination and freedom of choice.

When the compatibilist, on the other hand, says that I could have done otherwise than I did, e.g., by wearing the blue suit rather than the brown, all he means is that I could have worn the blue suit if I had wanted to. That is, my choice to wear the brown suit was free in the sense that it was what *I* wanted to do and not a decision imposed upon me by some circumstance external to my desires (like, for instance, the blue suit being away at the dry cleaners). According to Flew, this is all that we ordinarily mean when we say that we freely chose some course of action: We mean that our decision was determined solely by our own desires, beliefs, values, etc., and that nothing would have prevented us from deciding otherwise if those desires, beliefs, values, etc., had been different.[11]

The upshot is that on a compatibilist interpretation of 'could have done otherwise' our decisions could still be free—that is, they could still be *ours*—even if God has placed us in circumstances that cause us always to choose what is right. After all, it might be pointed out, we don't think we are interfering with our children's freedom to choose when we endeavor to mold their characters so that they will internalize our values and thereby come to base their choices on such values.

The compatibilist observes that our values, beliefs, desires, etc., are in very large measure determined by factors outside of our control. What I value, for instance, depends in large measure upon the society into which I was born, my upbringing, the schools I attended, the organizations of which I am a member, the friends I keep, the publications I read, and so forth. Of course, in a sense I do choose my own values. I choose them because they seem right to me. But what seems right to me is not a matter under my control. The same seems to hold for beliefs. If I had been born in the year 952 rather than 1952, I would doubtless have had a very different set of beliefs. Of course, I do sometimes choose to change my beliefs. However, this occurs when my old beliefs no longer seem right, and here too what seems right to me is not under my control.

To the extent that our values and convictions are outside of our control, the incompatibilist must regard as unfree any choices determined by such values and convictions. The incompatibilist, says Flew, thereby introduces a new understanding of what it means to choose freely—one that runs counter to the usage established by the paradigms of ordinary language. The incompatibilist therefore has the burden of defending his radical and seemingly implausible revision of ordinary usage. Flew does not think this burden has been met.

It appears, therefore, that Flew and Mackie have a strong argument against the FWD: God could have populated the world with beings who always freely choose the good. Such a world would lack many of the grievous evils the present one has but would not lack moral goodness or, seemingly, any other good great enough to justify the existence of moral evil. Hence, it seems that God could not have had a moral justification for not creating such a world. Mackie and Flew could thus claim to have met Pike's challenge and to have supplied the missing premise needed to disprove the existence of God.

PLANTINGA AND THE FREE WILL DEFENSE

Plantinga has devoted considerable space to the elaboration of his own version of the FWD.[12] He claims to meet the objections of Mackie and Flew and to demonstrate that there is no inconsistency in asserting that God exists and that evil exists. Indeed, he claims to demonstrate that there is no inconsistency in claiming both that God exists and that the world contains as much evil as it in fact does contain. We turn now to his arguments.

Plantinga evinces a distinct lack of patience when he deals with the compatibilist objection to the FWD. At one point he says of the objection:

> This objection to the Free Will Defense seems utterly implausible. One might as well claim that being in jail doesn't really limit one's freedom on the grounds that if one were *not* in jail, he'd be free to come and go as he pleases.[13]

But such a comment indicates that the compatibilist objection has been completely misunderstood. Indeed, compatibilism begins with the conviction that our paradigm cases of free choice—those decisions that we call free if we call any decisions free—are such that they are *not* determined by any such jaillike restrictions. The compatibilist recognizes as wholly free only those choices that are made when *nothing*—whether it is an external condition like being in jail or an internal one like having been hypnotized—interferes with our decision-making operations. Nevertheless, for compatibilists our decisions *are* determined; they are determined by what our wills desire, by what our consciences tell us is right, and by what our beliefs tell us is true.

Perhaps, and this is only a conjecture, Plantinga's impatience with compatibilism springs from the fact that he construes it as implying that our decisions are out of our control. But if something determined by *my* desires, *my* values, and *my* beliefs is not something properly described as "under my control," what *could* possibly fit that description? Of course, one's desires, values, and beliefs are not themselves fully under one's control—God, for instance, could have arranged for them to be other than they are. However, the fact that certain of my beliefs or values, say, have been determined by factors outside of my control doesn't make them any less *mine,* nor does it remove from my control the decisions I base on them. For example, my belief that the hypotenuse of a right triangle is shorter in length than the sum of the lengths of the other two sides is a belief of mine that is not under my control. I never chose to have this belief; it was pounded into my reluctant head by a high school geometry teacher. Nevertheless, it is now my belief, I can't rid myself of it, and I am responsible for any decisions I base on it, like cutting across campus rather than taking the longer sidewalk route.

To be fair, Plantinga admits that he fails to take compatabilism very seriously.[14] Such honesty is admirable, but it does not excuse the cavalier treatment of a position espoused by Locke, Leibniz, Hume, Mill, and other thinkers of similar rank. Of course, even thinkers of the front rank can be wrong, but their considered opinions usually merit more than a brusque dismissal.

Whatever the merits of compatibilism, however, Plantinga thinks that the whole issue can be sidestepped.[15] As he sees it, all he has to argue is that the incompatibilist notion of freedom is *possibly* exemplified, i.e., that the ability to make choices that are not causally determined *could* conceivably be the kind of freedom that humans possess. Plantinga further regards it as obviously possible that God might place such a high value on good acts done freely in the incompatibilist sense that he would create a world in which creatures possess such freedom even though they sometimes misuse it. Furthermore, if creatures do possess freedom in the incompatibilist sense, then even God cannot prevent them from making whatever wicked choices they do make without thereby destroying their freedom. Plantinga contends that if these possibilities are conceded, then it must also be conceded that God *might* have had a morally adequate justification for creating a world with evil in it.

For the sake of argument, Mackie concedes that human actions and choices might not be determined by antecedent sufficient causes. But, he asks:

> In what other ways might they come about? They might be purely random, subject to no cause and no explanation. Or there might be some element of randomness within limits set by prior causes. Or they might be brought about by events which are themselves subject only to statistical laws, such as those of quantum physics are supposed to be.[16]

However, if human choices are thus in some sense random, it now becomes difficult to see that they have any value at all, much less sufficient value to justify all the moral evils of the world. Hence, such an understanding of freedom seems to be useless for the FWD:

> For that defense requires that human free will should either be, or be necessary for, something of such great value that it outweighs the badness of such wrong choices as are made, and we can discern no

value in any of these kinds of complete or partial randomness. We can indeed discern value in freedoms of other sorts, for example in doing something because one so wishes, rather than through constraint or duress, or in choosing a pursuit because one values it, or in rationally weighing the merits and demerits of alternative courses of action. . . . But freedoms of all these, and all similar, sorts are entirely compatible with causal determinism, and *a fortiori,* what matters for our present purpose, with an agent's being antecedently such that he will do one thing rather than another.[17]

If our choices are merely random, then they are things that just happen to us rather than things that we do, and how could that be of any value to God?

Plantinga replies that Mackie has simply given no arguments to establish that randomness and causal determination are the only two alternatives. "Why," he asks in a review of Mackie's book, "shouldn't it be, for example, that I am not caused to write this review by forces outside my control and (even given the past causal history of the world) could have refrained from doing so, while nonetheless my action is not merely random?"[18]

But Mackie's point is precisely that until the incompatibilist notion of freedom has been clearly spelled out—until we know *what* it is for something to be neither determined nor random—we have no way of saying that it could be of any value to God. Perhaps there is some third category that falls between 'causally determined' and 'random' and perhaps human choices belong in that category. If so, however, the nature of that category needs to be spelled out clearly, and it needs to be explained why it would be of such value to God.

Suppose, for the time being, we concede that humans are free in the incompatibilist sense and that God might possibly place a high value on such freedom. How, then, should the FWD proceed? We must pause here to make a crucial distinction; we must distinguish between a 'defense' and a 'theodicy'.

The traditional theistic response to the problem of evil has been to offer a 'theodicy'. A theodicy is an attempt to explain why God permits evil. For instance, some people have held that God permits evil because evil helps to build character by giving us challenges to overcome. A 'defense', on the other hand, does not attempt to explain the ways of God. Some theists, such as Plantinga, do not think that an explanation can be given of why God permits evil.[19] Indeed, they deny that theists are under any obligation to offer such explanations. Their aim is the more modest one of showing that theists do not contradict themselves or otherwise fall into irrationality when they affirm both that God exists and that evil exists.

Plantinga, having stressed that the FWD is a defense and not a theodicy, now employs it to argue that theistic claims are not contradictory. To show that two statements do not contradict each other, it is sufficient to show that they might *possibly* both be true. It is not necessary to show that they are true or even that they have the slightest likelihood of being true. It can even be admitted that one or both are false. All that is necessary is to show that there is some possible state of affairs such that *if* that state of affairs were actual, then both statements would be true.

For instance, we know that it is false that human beings and dinosaurs lived at the same time. Nevertheless, there is no contradiction in holding both of the following assertions:

(a) Humans lived 80 million years ago.

(b) Dinosaurs lived 80 million years ago.

Though we know (a) to be false, it *might* have been true. After all, innumerable movies have depicted it as being true. Now suppose that one of those movies, instead of being just a movie, shows the way things actually were 80 million years ago. In that case, (a) and (b) *would* both be true. Hence, the statement '(a) and (b) are both true' is not a self-contradiction. Again, it doesn't matter that (a) is false. All that matters is that there is a possible state of affairs in which both of them are true.

Contrast this with the case when our two statements are the following:

(a) Humans lived 80 million years ago.

(c) No humans lived 80 million years ago.

Now there is no possible state of affairs in which (a) and (c) are both true. If one is true, the other can't be. No movie could ever depict them as both being true. Hence, it would be a self-contradiction to assert '(a) and (c) are both true'.

The above considerations give Plantinga the strategy he uses to argue that 'God exists' and 'Evil exists' are not contradictory.[20] That is, if he can show that there exists some possible state of affairs, no matter how farfetched or unlikely, in which 'God exists' and 'Evil exists' are both true, then he will have shown that these two assertions are not contradictory. Specifically, Plantinga believes that he can show that it is possible both that God exists and that God could not have created a world containing free creatures and no moral evil.

To show that two statements are consistent, i.e., that there is some possible state of affairs that contains both of them, we proceed as follows. Suppose that p and q are the two statements to be proven consistent. Now look for some other statement, r, that is clearly consistent with either p or q. Suppose that r is clearly consistent with p. Now if it can be shown that p and r taken together entail q, that is, that if p and r are both true, then q *must* be true, it will have shown that p and q are consistent. For instance, suppose that p is 'Dinosaurs lived 80 million years ago' and q is 'Humans lived 80 million years ago' and you want to prove p and q consistent. Let r be the statement 'Some of the dinosaurs living 80 million years ago included humans in their diet'. Now, clearly p and r are consistent. Further, if p and r are both true, q has to be true. Hence, we know that p and q are consistent statements.

For the FWD, the two statements we want to prove consistent are 'God exists' and 'Evil exists'. Plantinga proceeds by looking for a third statement that is clearly consistent with 'God exists' and that, in conjunction with 'God exists', entails the statement 'Evil exists'. One candidate for such a statement would be 'God created a world containing moral goodness and it was not within God's power to create a world containing moral good but no moral evil'.[21] Now if this last statement (let's call it R to avoid having to write it out each time) is consistent with 'God exists', then the conjunction of these two statements will entail the statement 'Evil exists'.

But *is* R consistent with 'God exists'? There seems to be a problem here. R says that God cannot create a world containing moral good but no moral evil. As we have seen, however, Mackie and Flew argue that God's omnipotence entails that He *could* create a world with moral good but no moral evil. If they are right, then R is *inconsistent* with God's existence and so cannot serve to show that 'God exists' and 'Evil exists' are consistent.

Plantinga must therefore show that R is consistent with the statement 'God exists'. To do this, he must show that it is possible that a world containing moral goodness but no moral evil cannot be created even by an omnipotent God. That is, he must show that there are some possible worlds that not even an omnipotent God could create and that among such worlds might be all worlds that contain moral good but no moral evil.[22]

What kind of possible world is such that not even an omnipotent God could create it? Before answering this question, we must get clear on the idea of a 'possible world'. The idea of a possible world is one that ought to be familiar to science fiction fans. Science fiction readers know that our universe is only one of many (perhaps infinitely many) *possible* universes. Even real science employs similar notions: One of the various interpretations of quantum mechanics, the "many worlds" interpretation, postulates the existence of an infinite number of "parallel" universes. Put roughly, a possible world is a total state of affairs (i.e., one that either contains or precludes every other possible state of affairs) that either actually exists, as in the case of the real world, or could have existed but doesn't.

Returning now to the question of what kind of possible world even an omnipotent God could not create, we must distinguish between two senses of 'create'. Actually, instead of using the word 'create' we shall follow Plantinga in using the word 'actualize' where actualize means 'causes to become actual'. The reason for preferring 'actualize' is that, strictly speaking, God does not create possibilities; they already exist. God's power consists in making possibilities actual.

God is said to actualize a state of affairs 'strongly' when he directly causes it. He is said to actualize a state of affairs 'weakly' when he creates free creatures whom he permits to bring about that state of affairs through their own free choices.[23]

Now clearly God can create any possible world that depends only on what he can strongly actualize. There are, for instance, indefinitely many worlds containing no free creatures that God could have strongly actualized. What, though, about those possible worlds that do contain free creatures (where 'free', don't forget, is understood in the incompatibilist sense)? In such a world the actualization of certain states of affairs will depend upon the choices of creatures rather than of God. This means that in such a world certain states of affairs would be outside of God's control, i.e., he will not be able to actualize them in either the strong or weak sense. For instance, God might create Adam and Eve and put them in the Garden of Eden. What God cannot do, claims Plantinga, is prevent Adam and Eve from freely choosing to sin should they decide to do so.[24] Whether they choose to sin is up to Adam and Eve, not God.

Plantinga elaborates on the above point by developing a fictitious example:

> Curley Smith, the mayor of Boston, is opposed to the proposed freeway route; it would require destruction of the Old North Church along with some other antiquated and structurally unsound buildings. L. B. Smedes, the director of highways, asks him whether he'd drop his opposition for $1 million. "Of course," he replies. "Would you do it for $2?" asks Smedes. "What do you take me for?" comes the indignant reply. "That's already established," smirks Smedes; "all that remains is to nail down your price." Smedes then offers him a bribe of $35,000; unwilling to break with the fine old traditions of Bay State politics, Curley accepts. Smedes then spends a sleepless night wondering whether he could have bought Curley for $20,000.[25]

Now Plantinga has us consider the following statement: 'If Smedes had offered Curley a bribe of $20,000, then he would have accepted it'. Statements of this sort are called 'counterfactual conditionals'. A conditional is any statement that has an 'if . . . then' form. A counterfactual conditional is one in which the antecedent clause (the clause that comes after the "if" and before the "then") asserts something contrary to fact (Curley was offered $35,000, not $20,000). Counterfactual conditionals assert that something *would* have taken place if something had happened other than what *did* happen.

Now Plantinga asks us to suppose that the counterfactual conditional above is true, i.e., that if Smedes had offered Curley $20,000, and all other circumstances were left as unchanged as possible, that Curley would have accepted the lesser bribe. Of course, Curley's decision to accept the bribe would be free; nothing would *make* him accept it. Hence, it is *possible* that Curley would refrain from taking the $20,000 bribe. Again, he would be perfectly free either to accept or to reject it, and so there will be possible (but nonactual) worlds in which Curley does reject the bribe. Nevertheless, if the counterfactual is true, it tells us that Curley would in fact have chosen to take the bribe.

Since it is possible (though in fact untrue) that Curley would have refused the $20,000 bribe had it been offered him, there seems to be a possible state of affairs that not even God could actualize. Namely, God could not actualize that state of affairs in which (1) Smedes offers Curley a $20,000 bribe, (2) Curley freely refuses that offer, and (3) every other circumstance is as close as possible to the real world.

But surely, it seems, this would pose no problem for an omnipotent God. All God would have to do is to change Curley's circumstances. Perhaps God could arrange for an investigative reporter to get wind of Smedes's bribery scheme and write front-page stories about it. In that case, Curley would never be offered the bribe and so would have no chance to accept it. In short, it seems that God could have put Curley in a different world. God would know in advance in which circumstances Curley would choose to commit evil and would simply omit such circumstances from the world. Hence, it appears that God could indeed have actualized a world populated with free creatures who never choose to sin.

However, says Plantinga, it might be the case that *every* possible world in which God could place Curley is such that if Curley is free to make *any* morally significant decisions, he will make at least one bad one.[26] That is, Curley might suffer from what Plantinga calls "transworld depravity"; Curley is so corrupt that he does at least one wrong thing in every world in which God could place him and in which he has morally significant freedom. In other words, God perhaps cannot weakly actualize a world in which Curley exists, has morally significant freedom, and always refrains from doing wrong acts.

Perhaps, then, it would be best if God simply didn't create Curley. After all, there are plenty of other possible persons with whom God could have populated the world. Why, for instance, did God not fill the world with beings who *would* always freely choose to do good? After all, as I mentioned earlier, hosts of angels are supposed to exist that never have and never will sin. Why didn't God just stop after creating the good angels?

Plantinga counters that it might be the case that every possible creature suffers from transworld depravity.[27] That is, it might be a property of every possible creature that in every possible world in which God can actualize that creature and endow it with morally significant freedom, that creature will commit at least one wrong.

Perhaps even the angels and archangels suffer from transworld depravity.[28]

Now if this is the case—and remember that Plantinga doesn't have to argue that it is, only that it *might* be—then it would be impossible for God to create a world containing moral goodness but no evil. Moral goodness requires the possession of freedom, and it might be the case that every free creature would do at least one wrong thing in every world in which God could have placed that creature.

Remember that statement R was 'God created a world containing moral good and it was not within God's power to create a world containing moral good but no moral evil'. Now it seems that Plantinga has shown it possible that God exists, that he created a world containing moral goodness, and that it was not possible for him to create a world containing moral good but no moral evil. Hence, it seems that Plantinga has shown that R and 'God exists' are consistent. If so, then, since R and 'God exists' together entail that 'Evil exists' is true, then Plantinga seems to have shown that 'God exists' and 'Evil exists' are consistent.

Since the train of Plantinga's thought may have been missed in this morass of technical detail, let us briefly summarize his argument. One assumption made by those who charge inconsistency is that God can actualize any logically possible world. However, it can be shown that there are some possible worlds that not even an omnipotent being can actualize. Now it might be the case that among those possible worlds that God cannot actualize are all those that contain moral good but no moral evil. Hence, it is clearly logically possible that God exists, that he created a world containing moral good, and that moral evil exists. Here, then, we have a possible state of affairs that contains both God's existence and the existence of moral evil. Since this is a possible state of affairs, there can be no contradiction in conjointly asserting that God exists and that moral evil exists.

What are we to make of Plantinga's argument? Has he proven 'God exists' and 'Evil exists' to be consistent? The answer to this question depends in part on whether the incompatibilist notion of freedom can be coherently expressed. Supposing that it can, such a notion of freedom might well entail other problems. For instance, Anthony Kenny has argued that prior to the world's creation not even God could know what free actions would be performed by creatures who possess freedom in the incompatibilist sense.[29] However, this seems to imply that God did not know what sort of world he was creating, since which world exists will depend in large measure on the choices of free creatures. But to say that God did not know which world he was creating seems to conflict with the traditional notions of omniscience that entail that God does have such knowledge.

The only reservations I have about Plantinga's arguments arise from a consideration of the devices he employs to extend his arguments to show that God's existence is compatible with evils of the sort found in the *real* world. This is a necessary task for Plantinga. After all, it is the evils of the *real* world that create a problem for theism, not the evils of some merely possible world. To show that God's existence is compatible with evil in the abstract is one thing; to show that it is compatible with evils of the sort that actually exist is quite another.

First, I'm not sure that he can successfully extend his arguments to cover natural evils. Natural evils, remember, are those, like earthquakes, floods, plagues, droughts, genetic disorders, insanity, and others that are not, or are often not, products of wicked human choice. How can the FWD be made to apply to evils that are not brought about by wicked human choices? Unless this difficulty is adequately addressed, Plantinga will not have shown that 'God exists' is consistent with 'Natural evil exists'.

Plantinga thinks that Satan and his minions might be responsible for natural evil.[30] That is, there might exist powerful, utterly malevolent nonhuman spirits who have rebelled against God and who now vent their hatred on his creation. Thus natural evils might be the result of the free choices of nonhuman spirits, and it is possible that it was not within God's power to create a better balance of moral good over moral evil with respect to the actions of nonhuman spirits.

Plantinga complains—justly I think—that his demon scenario has been unfairly scorned by those who consider it implausible, improbable, and wildly ad hoc.[31] It is all of those things, but this criticism is irrelevant when the question is one of logical consistency. To show that God's existence is compatible with the existence of natural evils, Plantinga only needs to show that it is *possible* that demons exist, that they cause natural evil of their own free will, and that God could not have created a better balance of moral good over moral evil with respect to nonhuman spirits.

But how is any of this even possible? What would it be like

to bring about natural evils? Natural evils are caused, so far as we can tell, by the same fundamental laws of nature that explain all other natural phenomena. Earthquakes are caused by the same tectonic processes that produce majestic mountain ranges; pathogens and parasites evolved according to the same laws as kittens and butter-flies; weather systems that bring balmy breezes to one region bring tornadoes to another. The causes of natural evil are thus so intimately involved with (and often identical to) the causes of all other natural phenomena that to cause natural evil, it would seem to be necessary to cause nature.

But in that case, what becomes of the doctrine of God as creator? At best we would seem to have a kind of dualism reminiscent of Manichaeism—a heretical movement of the late Roman Empire that viewed the cosmos as the creation of eternally opposed good and evil principles. If the demon scenario is thus inconsistent with the doctrine of God as the creator, it cannot be of any use to Plantinga, not even as a bare possibility.

Of course, if Plantinga were denied the demon scenario, he would simply begin the search for another scenario that would do the job. Furthermore, there is every reason to think he would succeed. If one is determined at all costs to show that two propositions are consistent, and if one is not concerned about how wildly implausible or ad hoc are the devices whereby such consistency is achieved, then one's efforts will very likely be rewarded.

A further difficulty with Plantinga's argument is his assumption that free will could have the sort of absolute value he thinks it might have. As we saw earlier, ordinary moral judgments do not grant such a value to the possession or employment of free will. For instance, if I knew that a terrorist, of his own free will, planned to plant a bomb on an airliner, I would feel obliged to do everything in my power to inhibit him from exercising his free will in that way. How then is it possible that God could be justified in allowing Satan to run amok? How is it consistent with the goodness of God *not* to have placed greater restrictions on Satan's freedom?

Nothing that I have said is intended to detract from Plantinga's achievement. I have questioned some of his premises and assumptions. However, I think that if all of Plantinga's premises and assumptions are granted, then he has indeed shown that 'God exists' and 'Evil exists' are consistent. I even think that, granted his premises and assumptions, he has proven that 'God exists' and that 'Evil of the kind, variety, and extent found in the real world exists' are consistent. The best thing we can say about a philosophical argument is that if we grant its basic premises and assumptions, then it accomplishes all it set out to do. Since Plantinga's argument does this, it is a major achievement in the philosophy of religion.

EVIL AND EVIDENCE

Let us try a different approach. Let us come down from the ethereal realm of possible worlds back to the real world. If we grant the success of Plantinga's argument, what he has shown is that God is *possibly* justified in allowing the existence of evil. However, for all that Plantinga has told us, it is equally possible that God is *not* justified in permitting the existence of evil. Suppose that we concede the logical possibility that God is justified in allowing evil. Suppose we even concede, again as a purely abstract possibility, that God might be justified in permitting as much evil as is found in the real world. By making such concessions we admit only that for every evil that exists, a sufficiently clever theist might be able to imagine a scenario, no matter how farfetched, wildly implausible, or outrageously ad hoc, that, if it were true, would justify God's permission of that evil. Such concessions do not in the least vitiate arguments that God is *in fact* unjustified in permitting either some or all of the world's evil.

Suppose that we phrase the problem of evil as an argument that some of the world's evils are in fact unjustified. That is, suppose we can point to certain evils and persuasively argue that a perfectly good and all-powerful being would not permit the existence of such evils. To reply to such an argument, it will not do to say merely that such evils are possibly justified. Such an argument must be refuted; it is not enough to point out that its conclusion is not a necessary truth.

The model for an argument of the sort we are looking for is found in a parable offered by Roland Puccetti:

> Suppose we are all tenants of a large apartment building and we meet to discuss common problems. It is clear that the building has many faults. Walls are crumbling, ceilings develop cracks, the heat is sometimes off in winter and on in the summer, the elevators are unreliable, etc. The general feeling is that our landlord, whom none of us has

ever seen, is either incompetent or selfishly indifferent to our fate.
Some tenants, however, rise to his defense. They say he *may* have
good reason for letting the buildings go on in this way, though when
pressed they can't suggest any which sound convincing to most of
us. Now what would we normally do if we saw no prospect of getting
a reasonable explanation in the future? Surely we wouldn't just sit
back and suspend judgment indefinitely. It is always *possible* that anyone
really had good reasons for what he did, or what he did not do.
Ignorance of possible motivation does not prevent us, in human affairs,
from making a decision about someone's moral qualities.[32]

The relevance of this parable to the problem of evil is obvious. Note
that Puccetti does not charge that defenders of the landlord contradict
themselves. He admits that the landlord could *possibly* have good
reasons for allowing the apartment to remain in such a deplorable
state. That is, it is possible to imagine a scenario that, if it were
true, would exonerate the landlord. Perhaps the landlord has to spend
all of his money repaying loan sharks and has none left over to
do the necessary repairs. Puccetti's point is that unless it can be shown
that the landlord *is* justified in not making urgent repairs (and not
just that he *might* be), the condition of the apartment provides
overwhelming evidence that he is either incompetent or selfishly
indifferent.

On the face of it, everything Puccetti says about the earthly
landlord applies all the more to the heavenly one. Surely the enormous
variety, extent, and magnitude of the evils found in the world place
a much greater burden of justification on the theist than the ramshackle
condition of the apartment places on a defender of Puccetti's landlord.
To get some idea of the magnitude of that burden, consider the
following: It has been estimated that fifteen thousand children die
each day of dehydration brought about by diarrhea caused by malnutrition.[33] Theists assure us that it would cost God no effort to
alleviate such suffering, yet over five million children die annually
from this *one* cause. Further, malnutrition is only one of innumerable sources of suffering. No mention has been made of the suffering
caused by warfare, genocide, crime, torture, poverty, oppression, dis-
crimination, infectious diseases, genetic disorders, mental illness, earthquakes, hurricanes, floods, accidents, fires, etc. Is it reasonable to
believe that all of these evils are justified? Is it rational to hold that
not one instance of all that suffering ought to have been eliminated

by a perfectly good and omnipotent being? It does indeed appear that theists have a lot of explaining to do.

Most theists would doubtless find the above paragraph far too hasty and presumptuous. It is easy to see how the disgraceful condition of an apartment building counts against the claim that the landlord is competent and concerned for his tenants' welfare. Is it quite so easy to see how the evils of the world, terrible as they may be, constitute prima facie evidence against theistic claims? Clearly, a landlord has certain obligations to his tenants; if he is negligent he is rightly condemned as incompetent or callous. But perhaps, so theists will say, we are forgetting what God said to Job out of the whirlwind. What right do we have to judge God? It is easy to identify evils that a landord, if he were competent and concerned for his tenants' welfare, would not allow to exist. Can we so readily identify a set of evils that we are equally sure God would not allow to exist?

This is a fair challenge, and it can be answered by turning to the theistic definition of 'God'. We have seen that God is conceived of as perfectly good, but what does 'perfect goodness' really mean? Well, *part* of what it means is surely that a perfectly good being will not bring an evil into existence unless there is a legitimate excuse or an adequate justification for doing so. What kinds of excuses can legitimately be made by those who bring evils into existence? It seems that only two types of excuses are possible: ignorance and powerlessness. We cannot blame people who cause evils out of ignorance (provided that they cannot be blamed for being in a state of ignorance). For instance, a mother who gives a prescribed drug to her child cannot be blamed if the child has a bad reaction to the medicine. Her intention was to do the child good and she had no idea that the medicine might do harm. Similarly, we cannot blame persons who do something harmful but who cannot help what they are doing. Mentally ill persons, for instance, are compelled to commit the bizarre acts that are symptoms of their illness. Such persons are to be pitied rather than condemned.

What would be an adequate justification for causing an evil? It might be the case that it is necessary to cause a certain evil in order to prevent an even greater evil. We have already seen that doctors might have to cause pain in order to prevent greater pain. There are also circumstances in which an evil must be caused in order to permit the realization of some higher good. For instance, an instructor might have to impose the pain of a difficult examination in order to ensure that students acquire needed knowledge. In this case, the goal of imparting knowledge is a great enough good to justify imposing the pain of a tough exam.

Put roughly, a perfectly good being will cause an evil only if (a) he does so out of ignorance, (b) he was powerless not to bring it about, (c) the evil was necessary to prevent an even greater evil, or (d) the evil was necessary in order to bring about a good that is great enough to justify that evil. We may express this more accurately and precisely as the following principle (P):

> (P): A perfectly good being will not knowingly bring about an evil e that was within its power not to bring about unless not bringing about e is a sufficient condition for one or both of the following results. (1) Another evil e′ is brought into being (or allowed to continue in existence) such that e′ is as bad as or worse than e. (2) The realization of some good g is prevented (or its existence is discontinued), where g, had it occurred (or had its existence been allowed to continue), would have been good enough to have justified the occurrence of e.

The upshot of principle (P) is that a perfectly good being will be excused for bringing about an unjustified evil only if he did so out of ignorance or was powerless not to bring it about. Further, the only adequate justification for bringing an evil into being is that not doing so will result in (1) and/or (2).

The excuse of ignorance is not available to God. God is traditionally defined as omniscient; "omniscient" means "all-knowing." For God to be omniscient means, roughly, that if anything is knowable, God knows it. Further, if God is all-powerful, what could possibly compel him to create an evil? Only logical necessity would seem to impose any limit on what God could create or refrain from creating. Thus, if God is the creator of the universe, every evil that exists will either have been strongly or weakly actualized by God.

Our principle (P) thus has to be modified slightly when applied to God. Hence, the following principle (P*) is needed to tell us what sort of evil God will not actualize ('actualize' will be taken to include both the strong and the weak senses):

(P*): A perfectly good, omniscient, omnipotent creator of the universe will not actualize an evil *e* unless the nonactualization of *e* *logically entails* one or both of the following. (1*) Another evil *e'* is actualized such that *e'* is as bad as or worse than *e*. (2*) Some good *g* is not actualized where *g*, had it been actualized, would have been good enough to have justified the actualization of *e*.

Let the name 'superfluous evil' be given to all evil that a perfectly good, omniscient, and omnipotent creator would not actualize. If, therefore, such a creator does exist, since all evil in the universe will have been actualized either strongly or weakly by that creator, there should presently be no superfluous evil in the universe. If, however, we discover examples of superfluous evil, we must conclude that no perfectly good, omniscient, and omnipotent creator exists. Hence, the identification of superfluous evil in the world will show that God does not exist.

It is quite easy, moreover, to find evils that give every appearance of being superfluous. That is, many of the evils in our experience could have been left unactualized seemingly without necessitating equally bad or worse evils or precluding justifying goods. For instance, it is very hard to see that some other great evil would have necessarily resulted or some great good would have become unrealizable if AIDS had never come into the world. The same thing applies to birth defects, such as spina bifida, and genetic disorders, such as Down's Syndrome. Would the overall goodness of the world have been diminished if these evils had never been? On the other hand, if God had not actualized these evils, would he have been logically compelled to actualize something just as bad or worse? The abundance of cases of prima facie superfluous evil thus provides very strong evidence against the existence of God.

THEISM AND THEODICY

Theists can reply to the above argument in either of two ways. They can deny that any of the world's evils are prima facie superfluous, or they can concede that certain of the world's evils initially *appear* superfluous but argue that there are adequate grounds for maintaining that none of them really *is* superfluous.

To say that the world's evils are not even prima facie superfluous amounts to saying that it is *obvious* why God permits evil. This is because those who cause or permit great pain and suffering are automatically censured unless their actions can be excused or justified. Parents who can offer no excuse for letting their children go cold and hungry are rightly condemned. A landlord who has no visible justification for allowing his apartment building to go to wrack and ruin is rightly blamed by his tenants. A government that imprisons its people without being able to show cause is rightly considered despotic. These examples show that some acts, by their very nature, demand justification.

God's permission of suffering therefore automatically creates the demand for an explanation of why he does so. This demand is not created by troublesome atheologians. It arises from some of the most fundamental features of moral discourse. Those features are illustrated in Puccetti's parable and other such paradigms of blame-fixing situations. What these paradigms reveal is that certain acts automatically merit censure unless there are adequate grounds for regarding them as excusable or justified. Undeserved pain and suffering are evil per se. To cause or permit them must be considered reprehensible unless there are grounds for regarding their causation as excusable or justifiable.

Of course, there are many cases in which someone is obviously justified in causing pain or suffering. A doctor is obviously justified in administering a needed inoculation. In that case, the pain of the inoculation doesn't even appear unjustified. On the other hand, if someone jabbed us with a needle for no apparent reason, we would have excellent grounds for demanding to know why (and for holding this person blameworthy unless an adequate explanation were forthcoming). To say that none of the world's evils are even prima facie unjustified must therefore be to say that, like the good doctor, God has an obvious reason for permitting them.

I don't know of any theists who claim that God's reasons for permitting evil are obvious to them. Plantinga, for instance, admits that God's reasons for allowing evil are unknown to him.[34]

Perhaps, then, theists will admit that some of the evils of the world appear unjustified, i.e., that they are prima facie superfluous. There are two ways to go from this point. The first is to provide, at least in outline, a plausible justification for God's permission of evil. That is, one option is to produce a theodicy. The second is to argue that *independent* grounds exist for asserting God's perfect goodness and that these grounds make it at least rational to assert God's goodness in the face of prima facie superfluous evil. Let us first examine the second option.

What sorts of independent grounds could there be for asserting God's perfect goodness in the face of apparently unjustified evil? A theist might believe in God on the basis of a purely a priori argument, like one of the modal versions of the ontological argument. Since the conclusion of such an argument would entail the existence of a morally perfect God, such an argument, if successful, would prove that all evils are justified. The problem is that such arguments have fared poorly under the merciless critical scrutiny they have received.[35] It is generally agreed, even among theistic philosophers, that no such argument *proves* God's existence. Whether any such argument even provides rational *grounds* for belief in God is highly debatable. Since there is no space here to delve into such arguments, I shall pass over them.

A posteriori arguments, like the cosmological and design arguments, are no help here. What good would it do to prove the existence of an Uncaused Cause or Great Designer so long as evils remain apparently unjustified? In such a case, these arguments, instead of being arguments for the existence of God, would seem to support the existence of something like Descartes's evil demon.

Most theists would probably give a more personal answer if asked how they can maintain the goodness of God in the face of so much evil. When troubled, they have gone to God in prayer and found their burdens lifted; when depressed, they have found inspiration in Scripture; when remorseful, they have found forgiveness; while enduring a crisis, they have felt a sustaining presence that carried them through. Some believers, like Elie Wiesel, have had their faith shattered by their encounter with radical evil.[36] Others have found their faith strengthened.[37] There doesn't seem to be any way to argue that either reaction is deluded or irrational.

The atheological argument from evil therefore should not be construed as claiming to prove that theism is incoherent, inconsistent, or in any other way a deluded or irrational belief. Indeed, the aim of such an argument should be to *persuade* rather than *compel*. Hence, the argument from evil need not be construed as an effort to *force* theists into unbelief. As Robert M. Adams puts it:

The atheological program (like the program of natural theology) need not be one of rational coercion. It might be a more modest project of rational persuasion, intended not to coerce but to attract the minds of theists and agnostics, or perhaps to shore up the unbelief of atheists. Theist and atheist can reason together without either trying to prove that the other has been foolish or irrational.[38]

Hence, those whose belief in the goodness of God is based on personal experiences of the sorts mentioned above need not fear that the argument from evil will prove their belief irrational. However, as we saw in chapter 1, many theists will not be satisfied merely to claim that their beliefs are rational; they will want to argue for the truth of theism. The personal sort of answer to the argument from evil is clearly inappropriate for such a purpose.

To argue for theism in the manner of Swinburne, which presently seems the most viable way of doing so, is to argue for theism as an explanatory hypothesis. Unless it can be shown that apparently superfluous evils are not genuinely superfluous, such evils will count as prima facie evidence against such a hypothesis. Hence, unless a purely a priori proof can be supplied (and it seems that none can), the case for theism must include at least plausible grounds for regarding the world's evils as justified. That is, since the existence of superfluous evil precludes the existence of God, arguments for theistic belief must be accompanied by arguments that apparently superfluous evils are not so in actuality. In short, the case for theism must include a theodicy.

Without an adequate theodicy, arguing for God's existence will be like arguing that the earth is flat. Vast quantities of contrary data will either have to be ignored or dealt with in an arbitrary and ad hoc fashion.

Further, the need for a theodicy often arises for reasons other than the exigencies of philosophical debate. "Faith seeking understanding" is the motto of many Christian philosophers. For many thoughtful Christians the encounter with apparently unjustifiable evil is the greatest challenge to faith. Hence, *some* theists, at least, feel that they need a theodicy. That is, when confronted with so many evils that, on the face of it, God could and should have prevented, they seek a plausible justification for such evils.

It must be emphasized that an adequate theodicy must do more than show that the world's evils are *possibly* justified; it must give plausible grounds for thinking that in fact they *are* justified. Consider natural evils. There are a great number of these that ostensibly could have been left unactualized without necessitating equal or worse evils or precluding justifying goods. Take Alzheimer's disease, for instance— the malady that causes the gradual deterioration of mental faculties until the sufferer is left with no mind at all, not even the ability to recognize close relatives. What would plausibly justify God's permission of maladies such as Alzheimer's? Talk of devils and demons, even if such talk served to solve the consistency problem, is of no use here. Until evidence is offered for the existence of such entities, their existence remains a mere possibility. As with Puccetti's landlord, God's actions cannot be justified by saying He *might* have a good reason for allowing evil; reasons must be given for saying that He *is* justified.

As noted at the beginning of this chapter, controversy over the problem of evil extends back over many centuries. During that time theists have offered many attempted theodicies. The Bible, for instance, sometimes speaks of evil as God's punishment for sins. The ravages of the Assyrians were thus seen as God's just punishment for the waywardness of Israel.[39]

Nowadays one seldom hears evil defended as God's punishment for sins (those who rail about AIDS as God's punishment of sexual perversion are pretty much limited to the lunatic fringe). Perhaps the general erosion of the concept of "sin" has something to do with this. Perhaps the sheer implausibility of such an argument has led to its decline. After all, can the sufferings of animals and newborn infants be explained as the just chastisements of an outraged deity?

Other arguments, though no better than the one just mentioned, remain very popular. When the problem of evil is presented in an undergraduate classroom, the most common response is the argument that evil is necessary to serve as a counterpart or contrast to good. This is an odd claim and a hard one to understand clearly. Perhaps its aim is to suggest that the attempt to make a universe in which everything is good would be like trying to make a universe in which everything is pink. In such a universe there would be no contrasting colors and hence no way to recognize that everything is pink.

However, if contrast is needed to recognize that a universe is pink, only the tiniest patch of nonpink color would be required to make the necessary contrast. Similarly, if evil were needed as a counterpart to good, only the tiniest bit would be needed and not the appalling amount actually found in the world. Indeed, in order to have the concept of evil it does not seem necessary that there actually be any evil. Surely an omnipotent God could give us that concept without having to create any actual evil. Finally, even if an all-pink universe could not be *recognized* as pink, there seems to be no reason that it could not actually *be* pink. Hence, the universe could be good even if the lack of contrasting evils prevented it from being recognized as good.

Let us turn to a more creditable effort. Richard Swinburne, like Plantinga, places great emphasis on the importance of human free will.[40] Swinburne begins by claiming that to have free will precludes God, however surreptitiously, from predetermining our actions.[41] What we do must, at least in part, be a matter of our own uncaused choices. Now it is at least plausible that God would allow humans a significant share in the creation of their own destinies. In order to give them that responsibility, he had to make them capable of making genuine choices.

Since some choices are good and others bad, humans can be truly free only if God allows them to make bad choices. Some of these bad choices will involve harm to oneself or others. Further, the greater the share God gives us in shaping our own destinies, the more power he must allow us to harm one another:

> He must for example not merely give men the power to bruise each other, but also give men the power to become heroin addicts, to persuade other men to become heroin addicts, and to drop atom bombs. A God who greatly limits the harm which men can do to each other greatly limits the control over their destiny which he gives to men— just as an over-protective parent who preserves his child from almost every possible physical or moral danger does not allow him to run his own life, and in turn to make through his own choice a difference in the lives of others.[42]

How great a share, then, should humans be allowed in the creation of their own destinies? Swinburne thinks that God would not allow us unlimited powers to harm one another, so He must draw a line somewhere:

> The free-will defense does not deny that there must be a limit to the amount of harm which a good God would allow men to do to others

deliberately or through negligence. Clearly in our world there is a limit to the amount of harm which men can suffer. Men only live for so long, and if you inflict too much pain on them during their lives they become unconscious. It is in no way obvious that the limit to human suffering inflicted by other men is drawn in the wrong place— that if there is a God, he has given men too great a control over their own destiny.[43]

The limit, Swinburne says, is not obviously drawn in the wrong place. Perhaps, though, someone undergoing the sort of torment he so coolly contemplates would be inclined to disagree. At any rate, the important thing to note here is that Swinburne only claims that the limits of human responsibility are not obviously drawn at the wrong place. He gives us no reason to think they are drawn in the *right* place; this will be important to recall later in the chapter.

Nevertheless, if God did establish the correct limits of human responsibility, this accounts for the existence of moral evil. But what about natural evil? What about floods, hurricanes, cancer, plagues, genetic disorders, earthquakes, and all the other natural phenomena that cause much human and animal suffering? How can the need for human responsibility justify the occurrence of evils independent of human agency? Surprisingly, argues Swinburne, the free-will defense also seems to provide a way of accounting for natural evil.[44]

To be truly responsible for our actions we must know that by making certain choices we will be bringing about particular results. For instance, someone can only choose to commit murder if he knows which actions will result in his victim's death. How does the murderer learn, e.g., that he can kill his victim by putting cyanide in the soup? He might learn it by being told that cyanide is deadly. But the person he learned it from must have learned it from someone else and that person in turn from someone else and so on. This chain cannot stretch back ad infinitum; there must have been a first cyanide poisoning in human history. Therefore, the first cyanide poisoner could not have learned the deadly results of ingesting the substance by observing or hearing about a previous cyanide murder. It can only have been learned by seeing or being told of someone suffering death due to the accidental ingestion of cyanide or similar poisons. Further, inductive inferences, such as that cyanide is poisonous, cannot be based on only a very few isolated occurrences. To give grounds for sure knowledge, accidental cyanide poisonings must have occurred with sufficient frequency to justify the inference.

The same holds for natural evils in general. They occur in order to inform us which evils we can cause, refrain from causing, prevent, or allow to occur. Swinburne does not flinch from the attempt to justify in this way even some of the most gruesome natural evils:

> Thus we know that rabies causes a terrible death. With this knowledge we have the possibility of preventing such death (e.g., by controlling the entry of pet animals into Britain), or of negligently allowing it to occur or even of deliberately causing it. Only with the knowledge of the effects of rabies are such possibilities ours. But for us to gain knowledge of the effect of rabies it is necessary that others die of rabies (when the rabies was not preventable by man), and be seen to have done so. Generally, we can only have the opportunity to prevent disease affecting ourselves or others or to neglect to do so, or the opportunity to spread disease deliberately (e.g., by indulging in biological warfare), if there are naturally occurring diseases. And men can only have the opportunity to prevent incurable diseases or to allow them to occur, if there are naturally occurring incurable diseases.[45]

Swinburne is quite aware that many large-scale natural disasters cannot presently be caused or prevented by human beings. Their justification lies in the fact that humans of the future may well be faced with momentous decisions that we presently are incapable of making. Future humans might, for example, have the choice of whether to move the Earth closer to the Sun, colonize Mars, greatly extend the human lifespan, or create new organisms in laboratories. Swinburne comments:

> But rational choices on these matters can only be made in the light of knowledge of the consequences of alternative actions. The *most* sure knowledge can come only from the records of the effects on men of natural disasters, and of naturally caused changes of environment and constitution. If men are knowingly to determine the fate of future generations through making such choices they can do so most surely by having knowledge of the disasters which have befallen past generations.[46]

Further, the long-range plans of present and future humans can also be guided by knowledge of the evolutionary history of life on earth. Hence, the whole history of nature "red in tooth and claw" serves to guide us in making responsible long-range decisions.

Finally, Swinburne considers whether God could have spared humans and animals the torment of natural evils by giving people noninductive knowledge of the consequences of their actions. According to Swinburne, this would require that God tell us out loud which results will be caused by which actions. However, this would have the bad effect of letting everyone know for certain that God exists and is constantly watching all that we do. The possession by everyone of such knowledge would result in a severe abridgment of human responsibility. We would no longer make good decisions and refrain from bad ones simply because we want to do what is virtuous. Rather, knowing that God is constantly watching over us, we would be good out of prudence to avoid punishment.

In making an evaluation of Swinburne's theodicy, I will focus on his treatment of natural evil. Swinburne's treatment must be lauded for its boldness in attempting to explain things that many will regard as patently inexplicable. How successful is Swinburne's theodicy with respect to natural evils? To make an evaluation we must recall the requirements of principle P*. The problem of natural evil can be solved only by showing that there are plausible reasons for holding that natural evil is not superfluous. That is, Swinburne must show that the nonactualization of natural evils would have entailed the actualization of worse (or equivalent) evils or the nonactualization of justifying goods. For Swinburne, the responsibility of humans for their own and others' destinies is the justifying good that could not be actualized if God had not actualized natural evils.

To succeed in justifying natural evils in this way, Swinburne must perform two tasks. First, he must show that it is not logically possible for humans to be given such responsibility without the actualization of natural evils. Second, he must give sound reasons for thinking that human responsibility is a great enough good to justify the natural evils that actually occur. Swinburne has failed in both of these tasks.

With respect to the first task, he is far too hasty in his dismissal of the possibility that God could give us noninductive knowledge of the consequences of our actions. According to Swinburne, God could only give us noninductive knowledge by saying things out loud to us. But surely if God exists, his resources are not nearly so limited as Swinburne imagines.

It is easy to think of a number of ways that God could impart noninductive knowledge without revealing his existence. Knowledge of the consequences of certain actions could be implanted in us at birth as innate ideas. This sort of knowledge could come to us in dreams or as sudden flashes of insight. Such innate ideas, dreams, and flashes of insight would then be just basic facts about our mental life, and there would be no impelling reason to think that they reveal the existence of God. Further, it seems likely that such innate ideas, dreams, or flashes of insight would only have to be given to a very few people. God would know in advance which individuals would commit evils if they knew about them. He could implant such knowledge in some of these persons and then allow them to commit the evils. Before long, enough of these evils would have been committed to justify ordinary inductive inferences about them. Then, so long as people retained the knowledge based on inductive inferences, it would be unnecessary to impart innate ideas, dreams, or flashes of insight.

Even if God did speak to us directly, how are we to recognize that the voice we hear is God's? Would we not be more likely to identify such a voice as belonging to a demon since it tempts us to do terrible acts? Further, even if we did recognize that God had spoken to us, this would not completely deprive us of individual responsibility. It is far from obvious that someone who is certain of God's existence will only do good and avoid evil out of prudence. Is the mystic, who claims to have experienced an immediate encounter with God, incapable of true virtue? Conversely, can it be safely predicted that self-interest will keep the zealous Christian, who is thoroughly convinced that God punishes sinners, from committing gross evils? Saint Francis in the first instance and Torquemada in the second show that the answer to both of these questions is no.

It appears that Swinburne has failed to give any good reasons for thinking that God could not have given us noninductive knowledge of the consequences of our actions. God could make us dream, give us crystal balls to gaze into, or send talking snakes into our gardens; all such methods would be preferable to the creation of natural evil.

Further, Swinburne overlooks the possibility of indirect *inductive* knowledge of such consequences. For instance, someone with enough knowledge of biology and chemistry would be aware that certain chemical processes are necessary for the continuation of life. That person could also know that the chemical properties of a substance are such that they would inhibit one of those chemical processes necessary for life and its continuation. All of this could be known without ever having witnessed an actual death due to the ingestion of that chemical. It seems, therefore, that humans could have both inductive and noninductive knowledge of the consequences of their actions, and so be fully responsible for those acts, even if natural evil had not been actualized.

Suppose, though, that Swinburne did succeed in showing that the nonactualization of certain natural evils, e.g., infectious diseases, would necessarily have resulted in an abridgment of human responsibility. He could then only defend God's actualization of infectious diseases by claiming that the abridgment of responsibility involved in their nonactualization would have been an evil as bad or worse than the diseases themselves.

The first thing to note about the above claim is simply that it militates against basic, widely shared moral intuitions. Is the vigilance of those who control the entry of pet animals into Britain, or even the heroism of a Louis Pasteur, a great enough good to justify the existence of rabies? It is hard to imagine that those whose lives are devoted to the conquest of disease, or to caring for its victims, would see their own efforts, laudable as they may be, as contributing to the justification of such evils. One cannot imagine Mother Teresa believing that it is better for there to be lepers for her to act compassionately toward than for there to be no lepers. The attitude that seems most consonant with true compassion is the wish that those whose suffering is being alleviated had never had to suffer at all.

Further, if natural evils are actually blessings in disguise, then we are in this respect too richly blessed. There are far, far too many instances of natural evil for human beings to even begin to take responsibility for all of them. Speculations about what human beings will be able to take responsibility for in the future are just that— speculations. In the meantime, it appears that human beings could have just as much responsibility as they do now if that responsibility were focused on a smaller number of evils. For instance, if there were only half the number of diseases that there now are, this would still be enough to keep doctors, researchers, and all other interested parties fully occupied for the foreseeable future.

Finally, some very strange consequences would appear to follow from investigating human responsibility with as high a value as Swinburne does. For instance, scientists working in recombinant DNA research would be justified in creating new plagues and releasing them into the environment. Millions might die from these plagues, but that should be more than counterbalanced by the great increase in human responsibility. Less radically, perhaps we should limit our efforts to controlling disease and alleviating its effects rather than trying to eliminate it. Think of the enormous potential for human responsibility that left the world with the conquest of smallpox. Think how much more would be lost if a cure for cancer were discovered. Perhaps, though, God in his goodness will send us new diseases, like AIDS, to make up for the ones we conquer.

Presumably, Swinburne would deny these alleged consequences of his argument. He would want to claim that God was justified in creating the diseases that He did, but that we would not be justified in creating new ones. Swinburne could argue this only by claiming that God has created the perfect balance between the evil of disease and the good of human responsibility. If God had actualized less disease, humans would have too little responsibility; if He had actualized more, there would have been superfluous evil.

It will be recalled that Swinburne only said that the limits of human responsibility were not obviously drawn at the *wrong* place; he gave us no reason whatsoever to think that the limit was drawn at exactly the *right* place. If no such reason can be given, the notion that the actual balance of the evil of disease and the good of human responsibility is the ideal one is a completely ad hoc hypothesis. Indeed, it amounts to no more than saying that the balance between natural evil and human responsibility *might* be the ideal one. But to argue that prima facie superfluous evils are not actually superfluous, it must be argued that the balance between natural evil and human responsibility is indeed the right one, not just that it possibly is. Hence, Swinburne's attempted theodicy is just as ad hoc as Plantinga's demon scenario.

Swinburne's theodicy has therefore failed with respect to natural evils. He has given us no reason to think that many such natural evils as earthquakes, disease, birth defects, volcanic eruptions, etc., are not actually superfluous.

CONCLUSIONS

What conclusions have we reached about the problem of evil? We have seen that it does not seem possible for atheologians to prove that theists are committed to a contradiction when they affirm both the existence of God and the existence of evil. Further, it does not seem possible to argue that belief in God is irrational in the face of so many inexplicable evils. As we saw, theists might have independent grounds for belief in God's goodness—grounds that make it *rational* to belief in God even if no explanation can be given for evil.

However, we have also seen that it is possible to define a class of evils that a perfectly good and omnipotent being would not actualize. We have also seen that it is easy to give numerous prima facie examples of such evils. Furthermore, the most sophisticated recent effort to provide a theodicy has been shown to lack merit. I therefore conclude that atheists have a strong argument to offer against the truth of theism. This argument may not be strong enough to convince all rational theists, but then, as R. M. Adams pointed out, this need not be the argument's aim. The argument's aim is to show that atheists can bear a burden of proof in their debates with theists. In meeting this aim I believe that the argument is entirely successful.

NOTES

1. Nelson Pike, "Hume on Evil," in *God and Evil,* ed. Nelson Pike (Englewood Cliffs, N.J.: Prentice-Hall, 1964), p. 88.
2. Ibid., p. 96.
3. See J. L. Mackie, "Evil and Omnipotence," in Pike, *God and Evil,* and chapter 9 of Mackie's *The Miracle of Theism* (Oxford, England: Clarendon Press, 1982). See also Flew's "Divine Omnipotence and Human Freedom" (hereafter abbreviated "DOHF"), in *New Essays in Philosophical Theology,* Antony Flew and Alasdair MacIntyre, eds. (New York: Macmillan, 1973).
4. Mackie, "Evil and Omnipotence," p. 56.
5. Mackie, *The Miracle of Theism,* p. 164.
6. Flew, "DOHF," pp. 149–51.
7. Ibid., pp. 149–50.
8. Such arguments reflect the great influence of the later Wittgenstein. One of the lessons of the *Philosophical Investigations* is that the meaning of an expression is determined by its use.

9. Flew, "DOHF," p. 149.

10. Ibid., p. 153.

11. Ibid., p. 150.

12. Plantinga's most accessible writings on the subject are in *God, Freedom, and Evil* (Grand Rapids, Mich.: Eerdmans, 1977), pp. 7–59.

13. Ibid., p. 32.

14. See James E. Tomberlin and Peter von Inwagen, eds. *Alvin Plantinga* (Dordrecht, Holland: D. Reidel, 1985), p. 372.

15. Ibid., pp. 371–72.

16. Mackie, *The Miracle of Theism*, pp. 168–69.

17. Ibid., p. 169.

18. Alvin Plantinga, "Is Theism Really a Miracle?" *Faith and Philosophy* (April 1986): 125.

19. Tomberlin and von Inwagen, *Alvin Plantinga*, p. 35.

20. Ibid. pp. 42–43.

21. I have conjoined Plantinga's statements (35) and (36) on page 54 of *God, Freedom, and Evil.*

22. Plantinga argues for this in *God, Freedom, and Evil*, pp. 34–53.

23. Tomberlin and von Inwagen, *Alvin Plantinga*, p. 49.

24. Ibid., pp. 48–49.

25. Plantinga, *God, Freedom, and Evil*, pp. 45–46.

26. Ibid., pp. 47–48.

27. Ibid., p. 48.

28. However, this does seem to contradict the orthodox view that some angels never have and never will sin.

29. Anthony Kenny, *The God of the Philosophers* (Oxford, England: Clarendon Press: 1979), p. 70.

30. Plantinga, *God, Freedom, and Evil*, p. 58.

31. Tomberlin and von Inwagen, *Alvin Plantinga*, p. 43.

32. Roland Puccetti, "The Concept of God," *Philosophical Quarterly* 14 (1964): 243.

33. Figure from UNICEF. Quoted by James Rachels in *The Elements of Moral Philosophy* (New York: Random House, 1986), p. 65.

34. Tomberlin and von Inwagen, *Alvin Plantinga*, p. 35.

35. See Mackie, *The Miracle of Theism*, pp. 41–63.

36. Elie Wiesel was fifteen years old when he was sent to Auschwitz. His first night there he witnessed the cremation of the bodies of children. Wiesel gives us a very powerful statement of how the experience of radical evil can destroy a profound faith:

Never shall I forget that night, the first night in camp, which has turned my life into one long night, seven times cursed and seven times sealed. Never shall I forget that smoke. Never shall I forget the little faces of the children, whose bodies I saw turned into wreaths of smoke beneath a silent blue sky. Never shall I forget those flames which consumed my faith forever. Never shall I forget that nocturnal silence which deprived me for all eternity of the desire to live. Never shall I forget those moments which murdered my God and my soul and turned my dreams into dust. Never shall I forget these things, even if I am condemned to live as long as God Himself. Never.

From Elie Wiesel, *Night* (New York: Avon Books, 1969), p. 44.

37. Consider Herman Wouk's fictional but very convincing portrait of Aaron Jastrow in *War and Remembrance* (New York: Simon and Schuster, 1978).

38. Robert M. Adams, "Plantinga on the Problem of Evil," in *Alvin Plantinga,* p. 240.

39. See Isa. 10:5. Even more notoriously, the book of Genesis says that the pain women suffer during childbirth is a punishment for the sin of Eve (Gen. 3:16).

40. See chapter 11 of Swinburne's *The Existence of God* (Oxford, England: Clarendon Press, 1979) and his article "Natural Evil," *The American Philosophical Quarterly* 15, no. 4 (October 1978).

41. Swinburne, "Natural Evil," p. 296.

42. Ibid.

43. Ibid..

44. Ibid., p. 299.

45. Ibid..

46. Ibid., pp. 299–300.

4

Conclusion

What conclusions do we draw from this brief study of the analytic philosophy of religion? First, I do not think it is possible to prove that belief in God is irrational. Zealous atheists may be disappointed in this, but there is no reason they should be. It is not the belief in God per se that is so offensive to the secular spirit. After all, Voltaire, Thomas Jefferson, and Tom Paine retained belief in a supreme Creator/Lawgiver. What rightly offends secular humanists is the bigotry, obscurantism, prudery, and persecuting zeal that all too often accompany theistic belief, especially in its particular institutional manifestations. With respect to "scientific" creationism; Vatican views on sex, birth control, and the status of women; official intolerance of gays and lesbians; the crusade against abortion; and fundamentalism in all of its forms, we can still shout with Voltaire "*Écrasez l'infâme!* (Crush the infamous thing!)."

Further, as we saw in chapter 1, just because atheists cannot *prove* theism irrational does not mean that they are unjustified in considering it so. For instance, it is perfectly rational for an atheist to hold that the Marxist or Freudian explanation of theistic belief is correct. The atheist is completely justified in regarding all of the alleged grounds for theism to be merely rationalizations for irrationally based beliefs. The fact that the atheist cannot prove this to the *theist's* satisfaction is irrelevant.

However, the most important question for the philosophy of religion is not whether belief in God is rational, but whether that belief is true. As we saw, progress on this latter issue cannot be expected unless theists and atheists are willing to seek out a common universe of discourse, with shared canons of rationality and premises accepted by both sides. Plantinga's Calvinist epistemology appears to rule out or at least greatly limit such a possibility. To insulate the grounds of theistic belief from criticism by declaring them properly basic is, in effect, to remove them from the realm of public discourse. Such a move insures that theists and atheists will begin with radically different paradigms of proper basicality and, in the absence of any shared criteria for adjudicating between such paradigms (criteria of the sort foundationalism claimed to provide), there is little hope for rational agreement. Hermetically sealed in incompatible and unbridgeable belief systems, theists and atheists would simply have to agree to disagree.

In such a case one wonders what use it would be to have a branch of philosophy called "the philosophy of religion." Theists might engage in philosophical theology, but debates between theists and atheists would be no more fruitful or meaningful than debates between, say, those who love opera and those who hate it.

Swinburne is to be lauded for attempting to bridge the gulf between theist and atheist. However, we have seen that his effort to produce an inductive version of the cosmological argument is a failure. Is there any hope for the arguments for the existence of God? Well, some physicists have recently raised the question of how we are to account for the apparent "fine tuning" of the universe.[1] In other words, physics shows that if some of the fundamental constants of natural law had been different by even the tiniest of increments, no universe, or at least none capable of supporting intelligent life, would have existed. Surely, some ask, when we consider the vast range of values those constants could conceivably have had, must not the chances that they would have just the right values (right for the production of creatures like us) be infinitesimal? Must we not postulate the existence of God to account for such a circumstance?

There is no room here to adequately develop and assess such an argument. In my opinion it is subject to the same sorts of criticisms that have devastated such arguments since the time of Hume. We simply are in no position to estimate the likelihood that one set of ultimate brute facts would hold rather than some other.

However, supposing that no new cogent theistic arguments can be given, one again wonders what is to become of the philosophy of religion. As we saw, in the forum of public debate over the truth of theism, it is the theist who must bear the burden of proof. Those who lack a belief have no responsibility to defend that lack unless there is some reason that they should believe. The longer theists are unable to meet that burden of proof, the less interested atheists will be in arguing about it. Atheistic apathy is likely to be encouraged when it is noted that Alvin Plantinga—the finest of theistic philosophers, in my view—expends vast labors of logic to prove that theism, at best, can only claim to break even with atheism.

A final conclusion of our study is that the problem of evil remains a vast and unsolved problem for theism. It is true that evil cannot be used to prove that theism is inconsistent or irrational. However, theists can offer no clue to explain the existence of vast quantities of apparently superfluous evil. Such evil needs to be explained if theists want to argue for the truth of theism. Without such an explanation it is no more possible to argue that God exists than it is possible to argue that the world is flat. In either case a hypothesis is offered that, at least without a host of ad hoc additions and gerrymandering of concepts, cannot account for the observed data.

The analytic philosophy of religion offers theists the cold comfort that their beliefs cannot be proven irrational. However, when it comes to philosophical argumentation about the truth of theism, game, set, and match go to the atheists.

NOTE

1. On the "fine tuning" of the universe see Paul Davies, *Superforce* (New York: Simon and Schuster, 1984), chapter 14.

Brief Bibliographical Essay

The purpose of this essay is to offer the reader guidance in the pursuit of further reading on the topics covered in this book. Those who want a more conventional introduction to the philosophy of religion should read John Hick's excellent *Philosophy of Religion* in the Prentice-Hall Foundations of Philosophy series (Englewood Cliffs, N.J.: 1963) or J. C. A. Gaskin's equally excellent *The Quest for Eternity* (New York: Penguin Books, 1984). Gaskin has also written the definitive work on Hume's philosophy of religion; see *Hume's Philosophy of Religion,* 2d ed. (Atlantic Highlands, N.J.: Humanities Press International, 1988). Indeed, there probably still is no better general introduction to the philosophy of religion than Hume's *Dialogues Concerning Natural Religion.* I prefer the Norman Kemp Smith edition (New York: Macmillan, 1986).

For those interested in the evidentialist challenge to theism, Hanson's essay is the best place to start; see Norwood Russell Hanson, "What I Don't Believe," in *What I Do Not Believe, and Other Essays,* ed. Stephen Toulmin and Harry Wolf (Dordrecht, Holland: D. Reidel, 1971). Anyone who thinks that philosophical prose must be dull, pedantic, turgid, or loaded with stupefying technicalities ought to read Hanson. Antony Flew is probably the most famous proponent of the evidentialist challenge. His essay "The Presumption of Atheism," in *God, Freedom, and Immortality* (Buffalo, N.Y.: Prometheus Books, 1984), is a clear and detailed statement of this challenge.

Plantinga's Calvinist epistemology is set out at considerable length in his essay "Reason and Belief in God," in *Faith and Rationality,* ed. Alvin Plantinga and Nicholas Wolterstorff (Notre Dame, Ind.: Notre Dame University Press, 1986). Plantinga has conveniently expressed the main lines of his argument in large print. The technical details are in small print and may be skipped over by beginners. A lucid and provocative counterpoint to Plantinga's view is found in Anthony Kenny's Brampton Lectures, published as *Faith and Reason* (New York: Columbia University Press, 1983).

The classical arguments for the existence of God get a thorough drubbing in J. L. Mackie's brilliant *The Miracle of Theism* (Oxford, England: The Clarendon Press, 1982), and in Antony Flew's splendid *God and Philosophy* (London: Hutchinson, 1966). Swinburne's attempted defense of certain of these arguments is found in his *The Existence of God* (Oxford, England: The Clarendon Press, 1979). Portions of this book might be accessible to beginners, but on the whole it would be a pretty tough read. Especially helpful in understanding Swinburne would be a knowledge of the probability calculus, Bayes's theorem, and other fundamentals of inductive logic. Such information is best gained from Brian Skyrms's *Choice and Chance,* 3d ed. (Belmont, Calif.: Wadsworth, 1986).

A fine critique of some of Swinburne's arguments is found in Anthony O'Hear's *Experience, Explanation, and Faith* (London: Routledge and Kegan Paul, 1984). O'Hear's book is also a very good introduction to the philosophy of religion, though it is a bit sophisticated for the beginning reader.

The classic statement of the problem of evil is found in parts 10 and 11 of Hume's *Dialogues.* A powerful recent statement is H. J. McCloskey's *God and Evil* (The Hague: Martinus Nijhoff, 1974). A challenging, concise, and admirably clear version of the argument from evil is found in B. C. Johnson's *The Atheist Debater's Handbook* (Buffalo, N.Y.: Prometheus Books, 1983).

Plantinga gives a very clear, and at times quite moving, statement of his views on the problem of evil in the "Self-Profile" section of *Alvin Plantinga,* ed. James E. Tomberlin and Peter van Inwagen (Dordrecht, Holland: D. Reidel, 1985). Unfortunately, even the simplified version of Plantinga's Free-Will Defense, in *God, Freedom, and*

Evil (Grand Rapids, Mich.: Eerdamns, 1974), is still quite technical. Nevertheless, Plantinga is a first-rate philosophical intellect and the austere beauty of his arguments should not be missed by those who are capable of appreciating them. For an authoritative overview of Plantinga's treatment of the problem of evil, see R. M. Adam's "Plantinga on the Problem of Evil," in *Alvin Plantinga.*

The standard work on the history of attempts to formulate an adequate theodicy is John Hick's *Evil and the God of Love* (London: Macmillan, 1966). This book also states Hick's own theodicy, which remains one of the most plausible efforts. Swinburne's theodicy is found in his *The Existence of God* and in his article "Natural Evil," *The American Philosophical Quarterly* 15, no. 4 (October 1978): 295–301. See also Swinburne's contribution to *Reason and Religion,* ed. Stuart C. Brown (Ithaca, N.Y.: Cornell University Press, 1977).

Index